YOU CAN'T LEAVE THE HOUSE NAKED

Copyright © 2023 Lindsey Bernay

All rights reserved. No part of this publication may be reproduced, distributed, or transmitted in any form or by any means, including photocopying, recording, or other electronic or mechanical methods, without the prior written permission of the publisher, except in the case of brief quotations embodied in critical reviews and certain other noncommercial uses permitted by copyright law. For permission requests, write to the publisher, addressed "Attention: Permissions Coordinator," at the address below.

No Such Word Publishing
info@lindseybernay.com

ISBN: 979-8-9893998-0-2 (paperback)
ISBN: 979-8-9893998-1-9 (ebook)

Library of Congress Control Number: 2023920640

Printed in New York, New York

Ordering Information:
Special discounts are available on quantity purchases by corporations, associations, and others. For details, contact info@lindseybernay.com

Unless otherwise indicated, all the names and descriptions of individuals in this book are either the product of the author's imagination or used in a fictitious manner. Any resemblance to actual persons, living or dead, or actual events is purely coincidental. Furthermore, the information contained within this book represents the views and opinions of the author only and no affiliate companies.

YOU CAN'T LEAVE THE HOUSE NAKED

**UNCOVER YOUR POWER
BY LIVING AND DRESSING ON PURPOSE**

LINDSEY BERNAY

This book is dedicated to my future self.

I love learning how to be her.

TABLE OF CONTENTS

PART 1: How to Live and Dress on Purpose 3

PART 2: Dress for Your Future Self 25

    DAY 1: The Naked Dream (Come True) 27

    DAY 2: You Are the Influencer of Your Life 37

        Lindsey's Tips: Eliminate the Excuses 49

    DAY 3: Your *Happy Closet* Begins Today 53

        Lindsey's Tips: Be Picky About Your Happy 63

    DAY 4: Stop Disappearing 65

    DAY 5: Boldly Fill the Universe 75

        Lindsey's Tips: Unsolicited Advice at the Halfway Point 84

    DAY 6: Thanks for the Memories 85

    DAY 7: A More Powerful Version of You 95

        Lindsey's Tips: Don't Tell Me To Change 102

    DAY 8: A Closet Full of Compliments 105

    DAY 9: JFDI - Just Freakin' Doing It 111

        Lindsey's Tips: Taking My Own Advice 118

    DAY 10: I'm With the Band 121

PART 3: The Purposeful, Successful, Fashionable You 127

Author's Note 133

Acknowledgments 135

About the Author 137

(MOVING) FOREWORD

What do you think when you hear the word "**Fashionable**"?

Do you want to put the book down and quickly walk away (before anyone sees you), as you think to yourself...

"Well, that's not for me and it never will be."

How about the word "**Purposeful**"? Too vague?

"**Successful**"? Maybe that one feels good. We all love a great success story...

But let's imagine these 3 words together, as a way to describe **YOU**.

The **PURPOSEFUL YOU** looks in the mirror today and knows the great possibilities ahead.

The **SUCCESSFUL YOU** is up for the adventure.

The **FASHIONABLE YOU** holds tight to the fierceness of what you stand for, trendy or not.

It's time to put yourself at the top of your to-do list, so let's go...

PART 1
HOW TO LIVE AND DRESS ON PURPOSE

HERE YOU ARE...

Your alarm goes off. You open your eyes. Your brain is foggy. You wish you had one more hour to rest and not have to think. One more hour of just "you time" (you're certain this would be the solution). Even five more minutes would be the exact five needed to feel ready to take on the day.

The sheer annoyance that you know this extra time isn't possible sends an ache down your bones and into your stomach. You roll out of bed, get yourself sorted, possibly make your family breakfast and ponder the idea of working out. After everyone else in your life is decently ready, you allot roughly two to five minutes to throw on some clothes and get out the door.

Sound at all familiar?

You enjoy your life, you like your job (mostly), you "prayed" for this every day when you were little. You are truly living your own version of your favorite '90s comedies, the highs and the lows. You have found some version of the elusive "happily ever after." Even if you don't have all your sh*t together or you're going through a bump in the road, you understand the fairly great life you have built.

So why, at times, does it seem to feel a bit more mundane than you'd hoped? Your days seem to feel more... ordinary, rather than extraordinary.

Something is missing. You can't quite pinpoint what it is.

I don't know the answer to that either. I am just a stylist, not a therapist.

J/K, I got you. I actually MAY know.

After more than two decades styling women, I have gotten to know the ins and outs of their demanding lives. I have dressed women for their major life events, game-changing interviews, kids' soccer games, and even through the overwhelming feeling of "needing to do it all."

I have seen how, as busy women, we get everyone else "dressed" first. We take care of all the people in our life, and we go last.

Our days are filled with messages coming at us from every direction. There is so much noise, our own voices have gotten muted in the shuffle. Our identity is entangled in our kids' lives, our partner's choices, our boss's thoughts.

Go here, do this, get it done.

Rarely do we create the mental bandwidth to welcome the opinion that matters most, OUR OWN.

We are told that we shouldn't take up space or that we should never be TOO MUCH. If we do decide to claim our territory, we seem to be spilling over into someone else's.

We love our life, but we are ready to *represent* what it means to put ourselves first. We are done paying rent in the story of our lives. We have a compelling urge within us to break free. Bust open our jackets, show our capes, and save ourselves.

We are *over* saving everyone else first.

Checkmate, game over.

I get all of these feelings. I have felt them myself. I feel them now.

I had to write this book. I used it as a way to discover how to re-engage with myself. And I have spent over 100,000 working hours with many women who were craving the power to do the same.

Within these pages, I can't fix all of life's frustrations. I'm good, but not that good. LOL

What I can do is help you redefine the foundation of your day and learn ways to show up for your world and for YOURSELF—First.

This is where my expertise lies. That is why you are here, to understand what it means to visually align with your purpose. I have seen incredible change emerge from a seemingly unexpected place—YOUR CLOSET.

As one of the top luxury stylists in the nation, I have worked with women at their highest and lowest of times. We have sat for hours discussing their lives, planning their futures, and the incredible possibilities ahead in the outfits we created.

I have styled them through their greatest stories of promotions, weddings, and parties. I have also stood with them through the outfits of divorce, betrayal, weight gain, hormone changes, and family issues.

You see, through the good and the bad, our clothing is there with us too. What we wore on a certain day hangs in our closet. It serves as a visual reminder of either a fond memory or proof of life's tougher moments.

Our clothes can haunt us every morning, staring back at us in ways we never noticed.

Maybe you never realized the power your clothing has. You open your closet, not recognizing that it no longer reflects who you are today. Begging the question...

Even though you have changed, has your closet stayed the same?

The thousands of brilliant women I have helped in the last 24 years have shown me what it means to have strength and courage in so many ways.

But at times, we sat there together, discussing how in some aspects of their life, they had somehow lost sight of what they needed, wanted, or felt they deserved.

Especially when it came to their clothing and how they showed up for their world.

Often, they were too busy to realize that this piece of them was missing.

They felt unsure of how to confidently show up for the important event, business meeting, exciting trip, or unexpected date night that was suddenly upon them.

They looked inside their closet and had no idea what to do with everything that was staring back at them.

It was almost always a backlogged catalog that represented who they once were: shirts still remaining from a carefree college girl, jeans from a pre-baby body, a dress from an evening marred by the memory of a broken promise. Clothing that was outdated, and unaligned with who they were today.

The clothing on their body was no longer connected to the mind and lifestyle they had evolved into.

They couldn't remember the last time they loved their outfit or the way they looked in their jeans. They couldn't recall feeling powerful enough for the big meeting or sexy enough to be noticed.

They were caught off guard in the story of their own life.

In a way, their sense of self had become as routine as their morning. They felt lost, unrecognizable—even from themselves. Sometimes it felt too heavy, or too soon to articulate. They wondered where else they had let their message be silent to the outside world.

As their stylist, I helped them reclaim their outward facing confidence and find joy in the magnificent feeling of being *seen*.

It had been a long time since many of them had known what it means to be seen. Sure, they wanted the family photos and loved how adorable their children were, proud to show them off.

But they seemed to dread the idea of showing their identity, the one we wear on the outside.

The one that speaks for us without saying a word—our clothing.

When did we lose sight of this form of self-expression? Did we forget how to have an outward identity because we are so busy with everything else? Do we think that people don't notice or don't care?

Where is our personal style? Where is the confidence to show up for ourselves?

Where did it all go?

We have been taught to believe that confidence must come from within. We must learn to love who we are, from the inside. I value this sentiment.

But actually, I *also* call BS on this.

Confidence CAN and SHOULD also come from the way we present our physical selves to the world, and NOT JUST because of who we are on the inside.

We have every right to "take up space" and BE SEEN.

And NOT only because of the values we stand for, but for the CONFIDENT way we represent them.

As you march into the world each day, you should be proud of the clothes you put on your body.

You can glow up, show up, and give a F##K too.

Getting dressed, every day, for yourself and WITH purpose is the foundation of your physical and psychological well-being.

How Dare You Be Into Yourself?

We have agreed that we deserve to get manicures, facials, and great highlights in our hair. Have a girls weekend, organize our pantries for fun, and learn how to contour like Kylie (Jenner, that is, in case you haven't been keeping up with the Kardashian-Jenner dynasty).

We subscribe to the notions of eating organic foods for nourishment, going to a fave workout class for physical and mental health, and even allotting time to scroll endlessly on Instagram.

I get that you do all that, and I love that for you.

But when was the last time you got dressed for a date night and actually liked the way you looked? When was the last time you got dressed to stand out without the fear of being judged by others?

When was the last time you felt you deserved or could be the best dressed person in the room? When was the last time you felt that your jeans fit your tush perfectly? How recently has your blouse fell against your body in a way that made you feel sensuous and confident? Seriously, when?

The modern movement of self-care has become a strong message in our society. Yet the notions of purposeful dressing and establishing a powerful, confident style identity somehow got left behind.

Why does it seem like dressing in a certain way makes you feel superficial, while all the other things on the self-care menu supposedly make you healthy and whole?

It's almost become more cool to be the woman in yoga pants than it is to be the well-dressed person in great jeans and a beautiful blouse. We believe that being "overdressed" means we are trying too hard or are too "into" ourselves.

How dare we be INTO ourselves!?

We worry about what other people will say. Will the women in yoga pants think you're overdressed? Will everyone think that *you think* you're better than them?

So instead, you sink into the sea of black spandex, since everyone else seems to be doing it. Your head spins at the mere thought of wearing a pair of jeans. It's MUCH easier to throw on the same old leggings, and not have to think.

It's safer to do that, than to confidently show up in an outfit that brings your soul to life. MAYBE you never realized that an outfit can awaken your spirit, OR that how you show up matters.

You have rationalized it as the fact that your daily style routine is "good enough." You have grown accustomed to your clothing habits; they feel safe and easy.

We are caught up in our lives and our FULL to-do lists. Who we are on the outside and getting all decked out for a trip to the grocery store actually seems silly. I get it. There are way bigger zucchinis to bake... This one's for the vegans who aren't in the practice of having "bigger fish to fry."

What I mean is, I know there are many big and important "fishes" out there in the world that need our attention.

Making a positive impact on other people and on our planet before we leave should be a top priority. I love learning and expanding my mind through brilliant podcasts and the incredible authors at our fingertips. We are here to discover who we are, and leave the planet a better place than when we arrived.

BUT, CUE THE MIC DROP...

Of course we should enrich our minds and make a difference in the world around us.

BUT we must also put on the armor and start showing up,

OUTWARDLY, as the capable, accomplished person we are on the inside.

It doesn't make you shallow to believe that the clothes you wear can brighten your mood and lift your spirits. It doesn't make you selfish to prioritize the way you dress, both for who you are today and where you want to be in the future.

I've helped hundreds of clients come to the same conclusion, and they are better for it.

Through the years I have seen my clients go after bigger jobs, embark on new relationships, make terrifying changes, and conquer the defeating feelings of "less than." I have watched them evolve into who they wanted to become.

I have witnessed the magnificence they created from the outside-in, when they learned to dress "ON PURPOSE."

Now, it's YOUR TURN...

This book has fallen into your hands. I am YOUR stylist, here to teach you how to dress with MORE intention. MORE courage to boldly take up space. MORE clarity towards your success and MORE joy for who you are—today.

I will give you the tools and exercises that make this feel possible.

These three thoughts are the foundation of the book. You can write this down, but no test later. Are you ready?

1. **Your day starts in your closet.**
2. **What you say to yourself in the morning sets the foundation for your day.**

3. **YOU CAN'T LEAVE THE HOUSE NAKED.**

Now, if you can leave the house naked, then I think you should stop reading this book and go frolic buoyantly about your day. That's great. But for those that must cover their tushes before entering a board room or PTA meeting, we shall forge ahead.

Who Are You Anyway, Lindsey?

As a luxury wardrobing stylist, I have dressed some of the world's most powerful and brilliant women. In my two decades of styling, I have seen every style, trend, and price point. I have a love and knowledge of clothing that ranges from affordable fashion to runway couture. I help my clients embrace not only their personal style, but their personal brand. I help them create their closets based not on designer names or price tags, but on their dreams, their joys, and their vision.

The magic of watching their transformation fuels my spirit. I look at the women I work with and I see their possibilities—not just for what they can wear, but for who they want to become.

I consider myself an artist, a fashion coach, and a lifestyle curator. I honor the personal and emotional relationships we all have with our bodies and minds. I understand intimately what it means to feel that you truly have nothing to wear, as you stare at piles of clothing each morning.

I also know what it means to hate the way you look both naked and in your clothing. I know how it feels to wonder how you are going to show up in this world, with the confidence and courage you need to make it through the day.

I have my own story and journey of learning how to live and dress on purpose. I have personally felt what it means to courageously step into my light and come out of the darkness. I have battled with myself many mornings, wondering how I will possibly find the strength to "show up" today.

There was a point in my life where every day felt like I was walking an uphill battle, in the snow, with flip-flops on.

There were many days I would ask myself, "Who did I let down today? Is it even possible for me to make it up to them?" I would lay in bed at night, thinking, "I am totally overwhelmed, and I'll never be able to do it all."

The ironic thing was, I was dressing women every day in the most beautiful clothing. And I couldn't even leave the house without feeling like a total wardrobe mess.

I made excuses. I told myself, "I don't have the money to shop like my clients." "I have to wear things from a certain store because I need to represent the brand." Or the worst one, "I will wear something more cute or flattering tomorrow. I probably won't see anyone today that really cares how I look."

But who *do* we see every day? Who never lets things slide, and rarely gives us a break? (No, not our families)... Ourselves. The most important person I was letting down was myself.

I knew I wasn't showing up in the way I wanted to. I knew that on the days I felt I had "dressed with purpose," I was a bolder, more expressive version of me.

I also knew that I owned everything I needed to be this person. I was living in the 20% safe side of my closet, rather than believing I could actually wear the clothes I had bought for "someday Lindsey."

I was aching to find both my voice and my own personal sense of style.

So much of my life had been about helping others learn how to dress and empower themselves that I had lost myself in the process.

And that's OK. I wouldn't change my career or life path. It helped make me who I am. But I was ready for a change, and I was ready to start showing up more purposefully FOR MYSELF.

If I Can Do It, You Can Do It

I haven't always been a fashionista. In fact, I don't really love that term. There is so much more to me than just fashion, which is why this book is my love language. You can be so many things. Not one word has to define you.

When I was a kid, I was absolutely not the best dressed at school. My parents only allowed me to shop at JCPenney or Mervyn's, which was fine, but I was merely consuming clothing.

Style identity was not something I even understood. From the ages of 11 to 19, I was just trying to figure out who I was. Clothes weren't that important to me. I thought that clothing was something you wore because you had to, not something that could empower you.

At that point, I was years away from knowing how to dress *with* purpose. And even further from understanding that power can come from both the outside of my body, and the inside of my soul, equally.

Throughout various times in my life, I was able to recognize when I didn't feel like myself in certain clothing. I also remember the few moments that I did feel confident under my layers of clothes. I will never forget my Bat Mitzvah dress and wanting to hold it so tightly, feeling like the luckiest girl in the world that I got to wear it.

I tell you this because, to this day, I care more about *how* clothing makes someone feel, and less about what the clothes actually are.

I am not concerned with what designer made them or the retailer where you purchased them. I'm not here to tell you to spend lavishly on the latest trends or even on classic, timeless pieces.

I am asking you to invest in yourself. Start your day on purpose, where it begins and ends, in your closet and with YOU.

Where Have You Been Hiding?

I have dedicated my life to helping humans create incredibly dynamic lives within the clothing that they wear. I have seen how clothing and the energy of clothes on your body can help you step into both your purpose and power.

On this journey with me, you will open the doors to your closet and see a new way to view those hangers staring back at you.

You will NO LONGER throw *whatever* seems clean or convenient on your body.

You will not say, "Better luck tomorrow" or "I won't really see anyone today, so it doesn't matter."

The reality is you DO see someone every day. You see YOURSELF.

You pass your reflection in a window as you walk down the street. You glance up at the mirror as you wash your hands and immediately criticize yourself for what you're wearing.

"Ugh, I look horrible in this."

"This shirt is so old."

"I hate these pants."

"What am I even wearing?"

It doesn't feel good. And it's not good for your confidence, your outlook, your attitude, or even your ability to do your job or interact with others. It holds you back in ways that you may not even realize.

When you don't feel confident, you want to hide.

When you think of the word "hide," what does it mean to you? How does it feel to not want to show a part of your body, express an opinion that you have, or stand up for something you believe in?

In the simplest of terms, hiding means concealing, locking up, burying.

Clothing is an easy way to hide because we can use it to help us disappear. We wear an all-black wardrobe to conceal our body. We throw on oversized sweaters, shirts, or pants that we believe no one will notice us in.

We have spent too much of our lives waiting for the right time to come out of hiding. It is time to bring yourself out of the shadows.

And now, you have one of America's top stylists by your side. I am holding your hand as you wake up each morning. If you normally approach your closet, drawers, or your racks of clothing with a feeling of dread, boredom, frustration, or indifference, please remember that

I am there with you.

I am there for you as you turn away, feeling defeated, and say to yourself...

"No, not today. I can't find anything to wear."

"I'm having a fat day."

"I'm too tired."

"I work from home anyway."

"I'm just running to the grocery store."

I am encouraging you to say this instead: *"Why NOT today?"*

I want to bring this message to the world. I have been able to help thousands of women identify why they feel like they are buying so much, yet still have nothing to wear.

I have shown them how to use clothing as a way to expand their life, powerfully and purposefully.

Now I am here with you. It's your turn.

The *Happy* Closet

You know what's annoying? The term "happy." It makes everyone that doesn't feel "happy" feel pretty crappy, pretty quickly. The term is a bit trite, almost juvenile.

Because as adults, happy is a relative term. Some of us are "happy enough." Or maybe you are "happy today," but yesterday really sucked. With all the ups and downs that life can bring, that word can make us feel, well, un-happy.

BUT... I do believe there is a place where the term "happy" can consistently live. And that is in your closet.

Our mind can't always be happy, and our body has its rough days.

But learning how to create a *Happy Closet* helps ensure that your morning and the day ahead are off to a much greater beginning.

Your time in the morning, standing nude in your closet, is one of the first interactions you have with yourself. Maybe your day begins by brushing your teeth. You glance in the mirror, and give yourself a few compliments, "Yesss girl! I'm having a good hair day." You glance at your reflection. Your eye makeup is on point. You love your new lip gloss. Things are moving along nicely.

Then you go to get dressed. You open your closet.

Instantly, it's screaming at you. "That doesn't fit you anymore. This doesn't look good on you. You had a horrible experience last time you wore that top. None of this is appropriate for what you're doing today."

So then you say to yourself, "I wish I could just wear leggings."

This does not feel good.

When you open the doors to your closet, it should be a part of the happiness and brilliance that you are. It should not be a reflection of an old version of you, or tell you that you're not good enough today.

Let's take the word *happy* and relate it to your closet AND your morning:

- » It's a place that welcomes you every day with an array of choices that make sense for you.
- » It helps you convey your message to the world.
- » It helps you become a more vibrant version of you, instantly.
- » It speaks to the visual parts of you that connect with others.
- » It's YOURS, something that helps define you.
- » It contributes to your purpose.
- » It's FUN, it's art in thread form.
- » It's the best YOU today, not who you promise to be 10 pounds from now.
- » It represents your greatest memories and all that's possible for your future.

A *Happy Closet* speaks to you when you open its doors. The pieces inside tell you how beautiful you are.

They remind you that you fit just right, into whatever you want to wear TODAY.

Your *Happy Closet* reminds you of some pretty freakin' awesome experiences in your life.

It says, "*You got this.*"

Your *Happy Closet* has your back—literally.

If you put this book into practice, you will be stepping into a closet (and a life) that's quite possibly the happiest it's ever been. You can and will feel sexy, confident and thrilled—not only on special occasions, but EVERY DAY.

How to Use This Book on Your Terms

This is a 10-day realization practice and a commitment to choosing YOU. I am going to teach you how to incorporate transformative styling techniques into your daily routine.

I get it... The battle with our closets, the challenges that life brings, and the sheer confusion of how to create a *Happy Closet* can feel overwhelming.

But we'll get there, together.

I call this a practice because, like anything you work at, you get better at doing it... if you practice. You get stronger when you work the muscle again and again.

You can read the book straight through and enjoy the stories of transformation. Or you can pace yourself, stopping to absorb a chapter one day at a time, completing the "Try This On" exercises as you go.

The exercises are meant to be contemplative and eye-opening, and should only take 5-10 minutes.

However you decide to read this book, my hope is that you will take it in, reflect, and see a new path forward.

The gift begins with you allotting the time for yourself. The change comes with the experience of doing it.

Perhaps, for the first time in years, you will look closely at yourself. It might pain you to realize how you haven't allowed yourself to be seen in a long time.

It might be difficult to accept that sinking into the background or struggling to feel confident has just become your way of life.

All I can say is, if you do this, if you read this book, in spite of how busy, overwhelmed or LOST you are, you will feel a connection to yourself. One that you may have been craving, whether you realized it or not.

You may want to give up. You may feel various levels of disconnection and frustration after three, five, or nine days. Your mind may start to tell you stories that seem real, because those dang habits are hard to break!

Your head will say, "No one cares what I am wearing."

Your body will say, "I deserve to feel comfortable."

Your ego will say, "Don't tell me what to do!"

Your exhaustion will say, "I have earned this break, so I am wearing my yoga pants again today. I will deal with this another day."

This is where the growth happens, on the days that are the hardest. When you feel overwhelmed, and you want to give up, that's your inner critic telling you that you aren't good enough.

It's telling you all sorts of stories that allow you to stay comfortable, rather than powerful.

You MUST push past this voice. Empower yourself with a new perspective. Use your potential to rise above your habits.

It's Time to Start Dressing for the Life You Want

This is it, the last stop on the train before the long-haul journey.

When you read the next chapter, you will begin stepping into the next level of who you are, just by turning the page.

I'm so into this for you.

So ask yourself this: "If not now, when?"

When you lose the weight that you feel has been holding you back?

When you finally have the time to prioritize yourself?

When you gather up the support of other people in your life?

If you wait for all of these days to come, you're denying the person you are today the enjoyment that may or may not happen in the future. You are missing out on what the current experience of TODAY can feel like.

That's why my advice to you is this: Do it now. If you wait for all the stars in your life to align before you begin to dress purposefully and with unyielding confidence, then you are denying the person you are TODAY the experience of stepping into all that is possible for you.

Don't waste another second of your precious life.

The goal of this book is to help you notice and shift away from the energy of "not caring." Or worse, thinking, "No one cares anyway." These are not the thoughts of trailblazers like you.

This is not the emotion of unstoppable people.

And you are unstoppable.

This is the beginning of your next level.

You just won the round. You are moving on. Let's go.

PART 2

DRESS FOR YOUR FUTURE SELF

DAY 1

THE NAKED DREAM (COME TRUE)

I once had a dream that I was walking up New York's Fifth Avenue, having the most enjoyable afternoon. The sun was shining, it was a gorgeous, chilly Fall day, and I was naked.

Well, I realized I was naked about halfway to Central Park. Then the dream turned into one of those nightmares where you are running but not getting anywhere. I was shook.

I woke up, clutching my Target pajamas and super grateful to be tucked away in my Park Avenue apartment.

I don't normally have dreams like that. I actually can't remember most of the things I dream about. Aside from when I was a teenager and used to wake up in a cold sweat after a nightmare about my best friend stealing my boyfriend.

Ugh, I know, but I can't get into that here.

Anyway, I looked up the meaning of the dream. According to Google, the most valued reference site, nakedness often reflects an individual's insecurities, a feeling of being exposed, or revealing our weakness.

Woah, that's some deepness.

Ironically, we also wear clothing to cover and hide our insecurities. We cover up, so no one can see our "flaws."

But what if our flaws are what make us whole? What if what we are trying to conceal under our clothing is actually what has made us strong and shows our perseverance?

What if we used our clothing to bring out our good, rather than hide the bad?

What if you dressed in a way that spotlighted all that was great about you, and that your intention was not to hide, but to highlight?

Are you writing your life story as you want it to be told? Showing up for yourself in a way that reflects your deepest desires? Are you dreaming of trips to Paris, big promotions, and exciting opportunities?

Or are you dreaming of being naked, worried about your worries and the way people see you?

Are you living life on autopilot, getting dressed in the morning with your cruise control on, and leaving the house as if the story of the day was already pre-written for you?

How much of your day is unintentionally lived and how much of your day do you do on purpose? How much of your day are you working to make your dreams come true, rather than forgetting that you ever even had them?

Let's start with your morning, where your routine begins.

Oh no... Is this where the monotony takes over, and where your dreams go to die?

I mean, you probably don't put an intense amount of thought into brushing your teeth. It's simply something you do because you would never leave the house without doing it.

There are so many things we do every day, things that just happen because we have done them for so long. They are embedded into who we are.

Brush your teeth, check.

Kids out the door, check.

Get to work on time, check.

Have you ever noticed how much of your days are filled with things you do out of habit versus on purpose?

Most days, I can get through an entire 10 hours without even realizing all I have experienced. It is wondrous that you can wake up in one city and fall asleep in another. It's incredible how many different people we encounter, emotions we feel, and things we can accomplish in a day. The human body and human existence are quite miraculous.

When you take the time to stop and notice the world around you, you begin to see this more clearly.

The age-old phrase, "Stop and smell the roses" means to literally stop, for a second. Look at your world, see your exceptional existence, notice yourself, and DO IT ON PURPOSE.

This is how you begin telling your new story, the dreamy one... and it begins in your closet. Because this is where your day starts.

What is Purposeful Dressing?

I understand that you are moving at 100 MPH, and your life is in overdrive. The last thing your mind can wrap its head around is worrying about what you are going to wear today and how to show up *on purpose* in your clothes.

I do not want to take this away from you. Instead, I want to teach you how to expand in spite of it.

What are small ways you can start to notice where you show up as present and perceptive, rather than routine and mundane?

Intentional. Purposeful. Dressing. These three words will change the way you shop, get dressed, and view yourself from here on out. Your closet should be your happy place that welcomes you each morning.

Your day should begin with a spark of power as you look in the mirror. When you start your day on purpose, your day becomes more purposeful.

Push past the feeling that you are being self-indulgent. Let's open your life up to what it could feel like to have a *Happy Closet*, something that's all about you.

Purposeful living and dressing starts in your closet, because this is where your day starts.

Each morning you are faced with things you HAVE to do. You have a big meeting. You have to meet someone for lunch. You have to work out. You have to run errands and get things done.

Have you stopped to ask yourself how you WANT to feel as you do those things?

- » I want to feel put together.
- » I want to know what it feels like to be confident in myself.
- » I want to feel cool.
- » I want to look "put together."
- » I want to have things I know how to wear!

It's wild to think that we rarely take the time to identify the WANT in our HAVE TO.

So we are going to start with that.

As you scan your closet today, choose how you WANT to feel. Don't just get dressed because you have to.

This may seem silly, but I want you to talk to your closet. Trust me, it's already speaking to you, friend.

For example, suppose that today you have decided you want to feel "cool."

Start with your jeans. Hold up a pair in your hands. Do these jeans qualify as "cool" to you? No? They make your tush look saggy! Put them back.

Now, put on the pair that you are afraid to wear but know you should.

Now hold up a shirt. Is this a shirt you wear all the time and it has sort of lost its luster? Yes? Put it back.

Grab the blouse that hasn't been touched and deserves to be

seen by the world.

It's time to pick a pair of shoes. Do they make your outfit feel complete? Or are you just grabbing whatever to get going?

Stand firm and confident in your shoes today. Wear something worthy of holding you up!

You do not have to sacrifice comfort for style. I wear sneakers every day. They make my outfit POP. I run circles around my to-do list while looking fab.

With your intentionally selected jeans, top, and shoes, you have begun to understand what it means to dress on purpose.

In My Shoes

I have a few "fashion pointers" up my bright pink sleeve that I have perfected throughout my career.

One of my favorites is first identifying my daily anchor piece.

I pick one item that I use to anchor and start my outfit. For me, my anchor piece is always my shoes. I am on my feet all day and if I am not comfortable, all I am thinking about is me, not you. And I want to be thinking about you or whoever the client is in front of me.

So, I always choose my shoes first.

Once I pick my happy shoe for the day, I move to a blouse that makes me feel chic and comfortable. Lastly, I choose my pants.

I organize my denim and trousers by fit and color. When reaching for which pant to wear, I know I want to push myself beyond my comfort zone BUT feel at ease with my choice all day.

As I am finalizing the details of my outfit, I quickly imagine a few scenarios. "What if I ran into my CEO today?" "What if walking down the street, I see someone I haven't seen in years. Will I feel good?"

This helps me make the decision to reach for the neutral, camel-colored chic pants, rather than the old, discolored black pair.

It now feels good to love the idea of who I may run into.

Your anchor piece is so valuable because you can use it as your jumping-off point. It can help the "dreaded" morning decision-making process run more smoothly. It also allows you to mentally review your day ahead.

It's important to ensure that your outfit fits the needs of your day. It doesn't make sense to pick a heavy silk shirt or stiletto heels if you are running around in 100-degree heat and humidity from 9 AM-6 PM.

I mean if it works for you, you do you, girl.

Personally, for me, I like to dress first for comfort and confidence. I then finalize my outfit choice with the style vibes I am going for that day.

What is your anchor piece today? Can you choose something first, and on purpose? Does it set the intention for your day in a more powerful way?

TRY THIS ON...
THE PURPOSEFUL NOW

If you are reading this chapter in the morning, I want you to notice from this moment on what you do on purpose today. If you are reading this book at the end of your day, please reflect on anything that may have felt purposeful to you. Jot down your responses in the notes in your phone, or in a journal you love. Take five minutes for yourself. Because if not now, when?

It can be anything that you did with intention and focus: making a meal, driving to work, calling a friend, even reading this book! Here are a few examples to get you started:

- » Waking up at a certain time
- » Jumping on social media
- » Choosing something specific to eat for breakfast
- » Brushing your hair before you leave the house
- » Getting gas for your car
- » Scheduling an important meeting

My hope is that over time, doing things on purpose will look more like this:

- » I picked a top that made my eyes look deeper and stand out more—on purpose.
- » I listened to a song that inspired me and reminded me of a happy time in my life—on purpose.

- » I made a list of things I was grateful for. Be it my cup of coffee, the sun shining, a warm bed to sleep in, the food on my plate, and my safe return home at the end of the day—on purpose.
- » I closed my eyes and imagined the new position at work I created for myself. I dreamed of something I could be in the future for one minute—on purpose.
- » I thanked myself in the mirror for being so beautiful, for being so me—on purpose.

◯ LET'S GET IT ON

Purposeful dressing begins with acceptance. Accept yourself as you are TODAY.

I want you to meet yourself where you are IN THIS MOMENT. Because today, you are exactly where you need to be.

You can lose 20 pounds, you can gain 20 pounds. You can have another baby. You can become a gym fanatic. You can start meditating every day. You can find the mental peace you have been searching for. You can plan to do all the things you hope and dream of. I believe that you will.

But today is about who you are now, in this moment, reading this sentence.

Maybe you are going through a tough emotional time, a divorce, or loss of someone close to you. Maybe you just can't handle one more thing on your plate. And even if you could, that thing can't be the decision of a better, more purposeful way to get dressed in the morning...

Here is a thought, you can make wardrobe and style changes when you have achieved all the goals and the dreams you have planned for yourself, your body, and your finances…

Or you can do it today.

If you continue to say you will reclaim your outward identity this spring, this fall, next summer, then you will have lost a whole season of possibility for yourself.

When we live in the past or put all our hope in the future, we rob ourselves of the incredible experience of deeply loving who we are right now.

Just by setting these intentions for yourself, you are making progress:

I choose to start dressing on purpose.

I choose not to let inconvenience or perfectionism stand in my way.

I choose to highlight what I love about myself.

I choose to have a *Happy Closet*, because this is where my day starts.

And I choose me.

Learning to dress and live ON PURPOSE is the next level of you. You are shedding your layers and making way for what's possible. You are doing it because YOU want to. Your "WHY" is for yourself because you have always known, deep down… you are destined for greatness.

DAY 2

YOU ARE THE INFLUENCER OF YOUR LIFE

We go to school from a young age to learn the facts of life. Mathematics, grammar, history, etc. As we get older, we hone in on specific skills. We choose colleges or career paths to focus on. We become specialists within our fields and begin to outsource the rest. We hire personal trainers to chisel our bodies, interior decorators to bring our spaces to life, and wealth advisors to keep us financially sound. You get the point.

But who taught you how to dress for your body, dress for confidence, or dress to feel good about yourself?

How do you, as the most important person in your life, learn to show up for yourself?

Most of us have never developed our own personal style. In many ways, we have been subliminally told it wasn't for us, or that we are "superficial" for caring about it.

I remember growing up believing that good style and fashion was only for skinny models, wealthy people who could afford it, movie stars, or those who knew how to chicly thrift shop.

Discovering our style identity seems to be at the bottom of our self-care list. Yet, there is an entire billion-dollar industry dedicated to selling clothes. There are aisles of magazines, famous TikTok-ers showing us "how to do it," and movie box office hits dedicated to stories of transformation and how your clothes can help shape your success. Think about movies like *Iron Man*, *Captain Marvel*, or Elle Woods in *Legally Blonde*. They are pretty bad-ass, their clothing included.

In the real world though, we don't necessarily give our clothes much thought or think of them as part of our superpowers. We scroll away, imagining that one day we may be "fab" like that blogger, but not today. Gotta run and live my life...

Have you ever heard someone thank their stylist at the Nobel Peace Prize ceremony, or even at the Academy Awards for that matter? Probably not, but all of these winners have shown up bigger and better at some point in their lives because of how they were dressed.

They changed the world in their daily armor, costume or not. It's time to believe that you can too. You are your own superhero. You are your own medal winner, showing up for everyone and everything at max speed daily.

What are you wearing to the awards ceremony celebrating your life?

Take Back Your Story

I didn't grow up around luxury clothing. We were your average middle-class family. I would sit at home, sifting through my TEEN magazine, feeling totally unaffiliated with that "fashion" world.

I didn't know what was truly possible with fashion until I stumbled into my first retail job at nineteen years old. It was a midline luxury store in Las Vegas. Most of my clients, even then, were powerful women. I dressed everyone from newscasters, and casino executives, to stay-at-home moms who wanted to feel good beyond the carpool lane.

It was then that I began to understand what fashion could be, and how it greatly impacts the quality of our mindset.

My clients would tell me stories about their day and how their outfit had helped shape its success. My goal has always been to help women build a wardrobe that sets the tone for who they are today, and identify ways to step into the future person they want to become.

I help women learn how to "show up" for themselves, and for their lives. Sometimes, uncovering their definition of "showing up bigger" is the first step in the styling process.

Often, we don't even know what that could mean, or haven't had the time to create the space for the "big" thoughts and dreams to come in.

We are in constant "go mode" with so much on our plates. (Truthfully, I'm exhausted just thinking about tackling my to-do list.)

When we aren't on the go, we just want to chill.

"Chilling" is something we feel we have earned at the close of a long, stimulating day.

With the addition of social media in our lives, we often end our days, "Netflix and scrolling."

We click through stories, and suddenly it feels like we will never be able to boldly "show up." Everyone else seems to be doing it so much better.

All of the good confidence from our day (if any) is gone with one click of an app.

The pictures and reels hit us hard. It feels like we may never have that influencer's body, budget, style, or the chic ease she has with herself and her life. The fit bloggers, luxury products, and seemingly perfect vacays appear. Gorgeous women who seem to be doing it all, so effortlessly.

As we lay in bed scrolling, we catch glimpses of people in couture clothing enjoying glorious travel destinations. They casually eat buttery croissants (as if they are calorie-free) and walk pristine beaches in their Hermes slides.

All of this noise can be quite discouraging.

Even long before the days of endless scrolling, glamour and the allure of the perfect life have been in our faces. We are trained to compare ourselves to others.

The feeling of inferiority and having to strive for perfection is deep in our subconscious.

Before social media, it was magazines that tested our confidence. If it wasn't magazines, it was the skinny models on the runway, or the captivating movie stars of years past. Before glamorous movie stars, we fawned over royalty and their court. Think Bridgerton in real time.

"Look up to me! I have it all!"

But we all know there is no such thing as "having it all," famous or not.

"Having it all" can mean you are juggling so many balls in the air that it's dizzying. And at times, scary. You're always agonizing how to keep everything afloat, or when it'll all come crashing down.

I found myself spending many nights with all these feelings taking over me. Convinced I would never be enough, for anyone, let alone myself.

I was stuck in the *humdrum* of life.

I didn't feel connected to my core desires. I realized that social media could be part of the issue.

I myself had lost how to show up "bigger." I didn't like the way this felt.

After a few months with this low-level energy, I set out on a quest to reframe the way I approached social media and viewed myself within its world.

I decided to use it as a way to find my voice, instead of just listening to everybody else's.

Today I am going to teach you how to take back the negative story of social media and learn how to use it to help create the future, expanded version of you.

It's time to start scrolling in the direction of your dreams. Learn how to empower yourself as the personal brand builder you are. No matter what your career or life path may currently be.

Bend and snap, we are moving on.

I Found a Way to Make Meaning of the Likes and Comments

It was March 2020 (insert your own memory here). I was totally out of sorts—maybe you can relate. The Covid pandemic had started, and I wasn't in a good place to even be thinking about clothing or styling. Yet, it had been my career and only source of income for 20-plus years. The world was on pause, and I certainly felt that fashion should be. Months later, when things slowly started to reopen, so did the luxury retail store I was working for.

After a few weeks, my phone started ringing. My clients were looking for inspiration during this heavy time. They wanted to know who to be and how to feel in this new world. "Comfortable," "cozy," and "at home" became the buzzwords. They were looking for clothes that helped them feel safe.

The tricky part was that I could no longer host clients within the beautifully curated walls of my styling suite. Emails felt too impersonal. Our inboxes were flooded with information and salesy communication. So, I turned to social media to find my voice, and my clients.

I started to research memes, videos, and posts that I thought my clients could relate to. I spent hours searching and saving the perfect message. I envisioned how I could recreate it as my own, tailored to my brand and customer.

I saw it as a tool to help build confidence for my clients, by starting with myself.

I was using the energy of social media in a liberating, creative way. This gave me the opportunity to see it as a research tool, rather than a toxic hole. I was able to reframe this traditionally negative space, and use it to connect with women around the world.

As a clothing stylist, I saw so many fun ways to show people how to dress and better their lives. To this day, when I am on a social platform, it is strictly for research purposes. What is trending? How can I make this cooler? How can I help someone with my next post?

When I start to feel myself spiral, comparing myself to others in my field or to people that feel way cooler than me, I simply shut down the app for a bit.

When this happens, I have forgotten the purpose and the story of my life. I need a break. AND THAT'S OK.

These feelings are normal. Social media is an entire world of "perfection," and the deeper you dive, the murkier the waters.

When I feel the overwhelm of "less than," I remind myself that my path is helping women live a more purposeful life through dressing. I quickly jump back to the accounts that help me stay on that track.

Over the course of a few years, I built an Instagram brand that represented me as the authority in my field. And before I truly felt like the authority, I used the platforms to help me appear to be.

Whether my following liked or commented on the content I created, I learned so much along the way. When I received a text saying I made someone laugh or solved their styling issue, I stepped into my confidence even more.

Whether you are a business owner, personal brand builder, OR stay-at-home mom, you can use social media in this way too.

You can create a message that speaks for you and becomes an instrumental part of your success and joy.

• Styling Stories •
HOW MARY BECAME THE INFLUENCER OF HER LIFE

Mary and I connected when she hired me to help with branding and styling for her business on social media. As a parent and education placement advisor, Mary was looking to expand her business to a new audience. She was ready to powerfully present her personal brand and company on a global, social platform.

We created new ways for Mary to present her message and intention. Her mission was to use social media to help parents, grow her business, and situate herself as the authority in her field.

We curated a wardrobe with shades and colors of her logo that would show up great on camera and also be easy for her to style, later on her own.

We hit a range of price points from Rent the Runway and The RealReal, to Saks Fifth Avenue. Now Mary had a foundational business wardrobe for travel, speaking engagements, important meetings, and social media.

When using a social platform for your business, or to get your point across, you have to show up as the most compelling version of you. You have to show up on purpose.

If you are growing your business or a personal dream, you can't shy away from the camera. It's impossible to do that and be a brand builder at the same time. We underestimate the visual impact we have on the world. You are more compelling when you represent yourself in a bigger, bolder way.

We spent six weeks creating content and outfits to help make Mary known to the world. This kind of energy was (and is) infectious. People see you doing something new, and they start to ask questions. You begin to stay top of mind. Humans love to spread the word, good or bad. "Oh, I saw this education tip Mary gave on Insta. You should teach your kid to do math like this... that's what Mary said."

Over the course of the year, Mary's business started to gain momentum on social media. First the client calls were small. Sometimes they just wanted to chat and understand what her business offered. Mary kept at it. She used her *Happy Closet* to keep filming, long after our six-week stint together was over.

Then one day I got a call from Mary. The kind of call that dreams are made of. A potential client in London had seen one of her educational videos on Instagram. They were impressed with her work and global reach. The client wanted to understand more about Mary's services. They were excited to have come across her page.

She was exactly what they were looking for as they researched their move across the pond. A record-breaking signed contract later, Mary had an incredible new client.

With a few international customers under her belt now, she could officially call herself an international parent and education placement advisor. She was the authority in her industry.

The path towards becoming the authority in your life and business begins with your mindset. If you do the work, show up consistently and let yourself evolve, you are already halfway there.

You have to believe it first, before you can ask anyone else to.

TRY THIS ON…

NOW BECOME THE OFFICIAL INFLUENCER OF YOUR OWN LIFE

You are going to use social media to research your style, define your point of view, and reclaim your power.

You will begin to discover your voice through fashion, *regardless of your pocketbook, taste level, and body type.*

Today you will take back the "noise" of social media and reframe it for YOU.

For those of you who love some good old deep diving into self-help and growth, this will come easy to you.

For the other half, I understand that this is not your comfort zone.

Personally, I have always had a hard time working on my future self. My brain gets all foggy when you ask me to envision myself five years from now. I am not great at seeing who I am in the future.

But I do know that I want to show up for myself. I do know that I want to be the most powerful and vibrant version of me; today, tomorrow, and 10 years from now.

So let's give this our all. Your future self is waiting.

Here is the plan: Today you can spend as much time on social media as you want. Call up the boss (you), and announce that there is a rebrand coming your way.

Find 10 photos on social media or the internet that represent the most excited, best dressed version of you. Screen grab these items and start an album titled:

"I am the influencer of my life."

Try to include these items in your album:

1. A coat or jacket you dream of having. A visual masterpiece for your eyes.
2. A pair of jeans you would love to throw on, regardless of size.
3. The cutest sneaker that you can't wait to wear.
4. The closet design on your bucket list.
5. A color palette that moves you (first one that comes to mind; don't overthink it.)
6. A "date night" or "girls night" outfit that gives you butterflies. (Yes, your clothes can give you butterflies, even if your date lacked them.)
7. A head-to-toe look that wows you—choose one professional and one casual look. A look that makes you feel like the authority in your field.
8. A fun bag that makes you excited to wear as arm candy. Imagine how powerful you feel as you enter a room wearing it. It says, I am here for a purpose and this bag is an extension of that energy. Focus less on designer logos, and more on color and detail.
9. A heel that you can stand, dance, and walk all night in. It has to be sexy and cute, BUT also the right heel height for your comfort level.

10. A matching pajama set that is your favorite color and is the perfect outfit to end your day with coziness and gratitude.

Please do not screen grab anything based solely on price or brand. That is not the focus of this activity and it's not relevant to the endgame here.

Today you are a little kid doing an art project, scrapbooking for your future self. This tech-forward vision board is the first step towards bringing your dreams to life.

Sometimes you have to see it first, to believe it's possible.

◊ DON'T GET SCHOOLED IN THE PROCESS

Social media platforms are a business and their job is to sell you a life that you may not have, but can "buy" into, through a series of clicks.

That is not the message for you today. The message is this.

Listen to me, loud and clear:

From now on, you are the influencer of YOUR life. You get to decide how you want to show up. You get to "like" yourself as you step into all you have imagined for your life. You are the Authority of YOU. Trust in what you know, and what you have to offer to everyone you meet.

We are all FOLLOWING YOU, so excited to see what you are doing to better serve yourself and this world. How epic is that?

Lindsey's Tips
ELIMINATE THE EXCUSES

As a stylist, I constantly hear these three statements from clients about their wardrobes:

1. *I don't have anything to wear.*
2. *I'm saving this outfit. I can't waste it on today because no one cares what I am wearing.*
3. *I just wear the same thing again and again. It may be boring, but it's easy and I need EASY.*

If these sound like you, it's time to turn up the volume of your purposeful life, and tune out the background noise.

Let me break them down for you here...

1. I don't have anything to wear.

You know the feeling. You're standing in the middle of your closet, scrutinizing your clothes, trying to carefully and wisely choose what to put on, because the day ahead really matters.

You might be meeting someone special for the first time, or making a presentation at work where something big hangs in the balance. You want to be able to sit and stand with ease, walk in and out of the room with confidence, flatter your figure, and highlight all your best qualities. And because you have about five minutes until you have to leave the house, all this has to magically come together FAST.

The clothes in your closet just hang there, offering no help. The seconds tick by and you know – you just KNOW – that you want to feel good today. You want to exude confidence like you see in the movies and effortless style like that girl on Instagram. Yet you have nothing to wear.

How could that be? You shop a bunch. In fact, you still have a few new boxes to open, yet nothing seems right. This is because our habits lead us down the same path, time and again. The habits have inadvertently picked out the same clothes from all the various stores around the world. Yes, I said it. It's the same clothes, only with nationwide shipping tacked on.

2. **I'm saving this outfit. I can't waste it on today because no one cares what I am wearing.**

Think back to a day where you told yourself that absolutely nothing special was going to happen. You won't run into anyone important. In fact, you'll barely leave the house, so you can throw on any old thing.

Why waste time, effort, and energy trying to put on something that looks good? See those joggers draped over the chair? They'll do just fine. And this wrinkled sweater? Sure, who cares? You pull on the clothes that don't matter, which is now really telling yourself that the day doesn't matter.

But life has a way of surprising you, doesn't it? You do run into someone, and you start to make excuses for yourself. You duck and hide, running the other way, because you don't want to be seen dressed the way you look today! Unexpectedly, you feel unprepared for the day you're actually living, a day when you could have shown up gloriously, purposefully.

My friends, we are done with that. Today is the day (a freakin' fabulous day) to face yourself and anything or anyone that may cross your path.

3. **I just wear the same thing again and again. It may be boring, but it's easy and I need EASY.**

You do it. I've done it. We have all been there. Wearing the same things over and over again because they fit, they're comfortable, and they're easy. These are the items that appear in your outfit rotations so frequently they feel like old friends. Oh, hello black V-neck T-shirt. Yes, it's that time again, you're up.

Routines become part of our lives for one reason—they're predictable. We rely on them because they give us a sense of familiarity, a kind of comfort, a little bit of control in the chaos. They feel safe, free of risk. But the flip side is that routines also dull our senses. Once embedded into our lives, we stop questioning them and then they become HABITS. They lull us into complacency. Routines are a way of putting ourselves on autopilot.

Habits can keep us safe, but habits also lead us to "play small." You probably won't find your life's passion being stuck in a routine, allowing your habits to define you, or thinking that anything about you is "good enough."

These habits can be where nothing new, bold, or creative happens. We let a little bit of ourselves, our imaginative edge, slip away when we decide to dim our light.

The clothes you put on are part of those habits. They are a main ingredient in your secret sauce, and the magical finishing touch of YOU. It is a WHOLE you. A GREAT you.

No matter how you feel today. Reading this book, learning the tools, and having a stylist (me), can help stop this negative self-talk.

You are worthy of being seen by the outside world in a bigger way. That's why you are here. I got you.

Let's break free of these habits, together.

DAY 3

YOUR *HAPPY CLOSET* BEGINS TODAY

Open it up, friend. Have a look. What do you see? What's in there? What's worn on repeat? What has been forgotten?

What is your closet filled with? Is it an array of simple shirts and blue jeans? Do you have several black trousers, cozy jackets, delicious sweaters, stiletto heels, or smart shoes? Do your drawers have a range of old underwear, new underwear, concert T-shirts, jeans from last week, or jeans from 12 years ago? Are you a minimalist with just a few things? Whatever it is, that's great. For now... (Dun, Dun, Duuuun. Cue foreshadowing music here.)

You are going to take a big step into your closet and uncover if the clothing inside represents the current expression of who you are and how you want to show up—on the *outside*.

Are you holding onto items that no longer serve you? Don't fit you? Things you haven't worn in so long, or ever?

Are you clutching onto pieces that represent a vacation purchase you never actually wore, or a sentimental gift that you never really liked? Do you have outfits you swear you'll wear when you lose those fifteen pounds?

Do you allow items to stay in your closet that bring up bad memories? Perhaps echoing difficult memories in your life, "I wore this when I was my heaviest." "This is when I was trying for a baby, with no luck." "This is when I failed the bar exam." "This is when I was sad or lonely."

Why do we hold onto things that don't deserve our energy anymore? Why is it hard to let go of our bad buys? Why can't we say farewell to the failed style, or pilly, outdated version of us?

It could mean that we hate to admit defeat, and be forced to wave the white flag. It's hard to admit to ourselves that we might have made a bad choice.

I get a lot of negative messages throughout the day already. The last place I really need to hear it is from myself, in my closet, just as I am trying to leave the house on time. No thank you.

What if your closet could be *happy*? What if you opened its doors, and just like in the movies, it smiled at you and said, "Good morning, you ravishing, brilliant, sexy beast of a human!"?

I bet your morning would start out a little more lovely if you didn't hear:

"That doesn't fit."

"Why did you buy that?"

"Ewww."

"Not today."

"Ugh, that shirt again?"

I think your day would be a bit brighter if you heard words of delight rather than dread. That is the feeling I want you to have. Because you deserve sheer delight.

I want you to get real comfortable saying these words to your closet: *It's not you, it's me.*

- » I won't wear this anymore.
- » I don't like that anymore.
- » I don't want to wear this, ever.
- » You don't make me happy.
- » This fabric gives me the "icks."
- » It's ok for me to give up on you.
- » I am the perfect size today.

It's not you, it's me. I've changed.

We are constantly evolving. Everything from our taste buds and our eyesight, to our favorite restaurants and the books we like to read. We are ever-changing.

You are not the person you were yesterday, let alone a year, or five years ago.

You may say, "Nope, I am the same." Nothing really seems THAT different.

Let me tell you a beautiful fact: You have changed. You are changing. You are living on purpose.

Starting with your closet, and starting today, you are going to begin your process of evolution. You can't leave the house naked. Wherever the road may take you, you'll need clothes.

• Styling Stories •
DON'T DOUBLE DOWN

Dana was headed on a magical trip to Italy, and she couldn't wait to shop. The moment she arrived, she hit the ground running. She roamed the streets of Rome, as if she herself were the original fashionista creating the couture. She told her daughter, "I want to buy something awesome and different when we arrive in Florence."

I can relate to Dana. Shopping on vacation is so fun. For me, it's like money isn't real. I find that to be especially true when the currency is different. Even with a terrible exchange rate, I lose all concept of money. Vacay shopping feeds your soul, even if it eats away at your pocketbook. What can I say, I'm a sucker for a bag and a baguette.

Then you return home from your trip, and all the spent cash and crushed croissants are back in reality land. I don't even mean the part when the bill comes. The regretful feeling can begin when you start to unpack your suitcase. The feeling is instantly, "What was I thinking? Who bought this?" "There is no way I am going to actually wear this."

"Vacation You" was perhaps way more adventurous than "Real-life You."

Dana was thrilled with the long, suede, fringe, trench coat she had bought at the fab boutique in Florence. It had that leather smell that makes you feel rich just being in its presence. The stylist in the boutique had told her the history of the leather maker, the tailor who crafted it, AND the origin of the leather.

Oh the story seemed as magical as the jacket itself. It was embroidered down the back with bold colors like emerald green, raspberry, and coral.

It was more than Dana had wanted to spend. But how could she pass it up? It was a memory, a moment. Vacation Dana NEEDED this jacket. It was perfect for dinners, or casual girls lunches paired with flats. You know, Dana was going to wear it ALL the time.

As Dana unpacked, she was still happy with her Florence purchase. It was summer in LA, so it was too hot to wear it now. But she swore as soon as the weather turned cooler, it would have its moment. Summer came and went. Then fall approached, but the right event still hadn't popped up in Dana's calendar.

That's ok, she thought. "Christmas. I will wear it for the holidays." As the ball dropped on New Years Eve, no leather fringe coat was worn.

A whole year passed. Every time Dana opened her closet, she saw the coat. She saw the reminder of that huge Italian expense. She started to notice that feeling in her gut telling her that she probably won't wear the coat. Each time her eyes fell on the jacket, nicely tucked away, she saw something about it she actually didn't love. She didn't know how to style it. The length was a tiny bit long. It didn't really have an LA vibe. It didn't seem to fit her lifestyle. The collar really wasn't her fave, and she actually didn't like the color coral at all.

This coat was not making Dana very happy. In fact, it made her sad. It didn't feel good to open her closet and be reminded of her expensive mistake. The jacket had set her back a bit, and this made her want to hold onto it even tighter. She had mostly lost interest in wearing it, but giving it away or selling it for a discount would for sure feel worse! She would rather force herself to wear it, no matter how many more months that took.

Then Dana got an idea. She was going to take the jacket to her local tailor and have it shortened. Certainly she would wear it more if it was shorter and felt a little less like a "whole situation."

Dana called me, excited to tell me the news. She had been one of my clients for a few years now, and we had talked about this leather coat several times. Whenever I had suggested she sell it, she would look at me like I had 14 eyes. "No! I will wear it someday!" When I suggested she move it to a different closet so she didn't have to see it every day, she said, "But then I will forget I have it and probably miss out on the perfect moment to wear it. I need to see it to remind myself to wear it!"

Trust me, she did not need to see it to be reminded to wear it.

"Lindsey," Dana said. "You remember that tan suede coat I got in Florence?"

"Yes, Dana, I will never forget that coat," I replied.

"I found a tailor who is going to shorten it. I'm sure I'll wear it more often if it's shorter," she happily told me.

"Ok Dana, that's an idea. How much is the tailoring going to cost to shorten a piece like that?" I asked.

The phone was silent for a few seconds...

"$650."

Another stretch of silence... Vacation Dana was trying to negotiate with real-life Dana, and she needed to be stopped.

Don't Double Down.

Spending more money on something that already has the stigma of not being wearable has a much higher chance of never being worn.

Even if you make the changes you think it needs, you are now double invested in a piece that clearly doesn't call to you. If it did, you would have worn it. You would have found a way, a time, a place. I promise.

It's kind of like what they say in the dating or job world, "No response is a response." When someone doesn't call you, you're not their priority. Harsh but true advice.

Sadly, you have tried to date this piece or pieces in your closet and they just aren't for you. It's ok to move on. The sooner you recognize this, the easier it is to invest in the pieces that you do want to frolic in the park with, and to stop buying the things that sit idle with no personality.

When you notice what makes you *happy*, in your *closet*, on your body, and even in your daily life, you will attract more of these things. You begin to build a *Happy Closet* by investing in yourself. When you stop consuming, and instead start collecting pieces that smile back at you, you are one step closer to your *happy*.

TRY THIS ON...
LET'S SORT IT OUT

Looking at your closet as you read this, let's examine it on a cellular level. This isn't organic chemistry, but let's give it our all as if it were. As you approach this, stay focused on the current season where you live. So if it's cold or chilly, focus on winter-forward pieces. If it's sunny and warm, focus on spring or summer. Gear your questions towards these items.

Look for a piece you haven't worn for six months to a year. Pull out THE FIRST item that comes to mind. Do not overthink it. You can pull out more than one item if you'd like, but I want you to focus on what initially comes to mind. First instincts are about to be refined here...

- » When was the last time you wore this item?
- » Where did you go?
- » How did wearing it make you feel?
- » Did you have a fun or successful experience when wearing it?
- » Why haven't you worn it since? (Please note: If you just had a baby, this exercise needs to be about pre-pregnancy gear, or come back to this in one year.)
- » Does it have sentimental value?
- » Is there someone you can give this to? Someone who will absolutely love and enjoy this item? Could you make someone's day by giving it to them?

Here's something to consider when you look into your closet and see items of clothing that are deeply meaningful to you. I love keeping special pieces that remind me of moments in my life. From trips I have taken (think Vacation Dana), or the items I plan to pass down for generations. Think of the items in your closet that are filled with nostalgia for you. Gifts from your husband or children. Items that a parent or another relative may have given you as keepsakes. If the item is sentimental, try moving it to a special box labeled "MEMORY CLOTHES."

These cherished items, no matter how lovely, do not belong in your closet if you don't regularly wear them. They take up physical and mental space for you. They make it seem like you have more options to choose from than you actually do. It feeds into that feeling, "I have all these clothes and nothing to wear."

The only items allowed in your closet are the ones you can wear right now. Your closet should not be cluttered with things that have a backstory. Unless that backstory can be worn again sooner than later.

Having these things in your closet may keep you from adding items that are actually wearable and that make you feel powerful TODAY. We don't need seat fillers; save those for the Academy Awards Show stand-ins.

◎ THE FACTS OF LIFE

Sometimes, it is not just our memories that are holding us back. We have deeply meaningful stories and truths we feel about our body and weight. This may be hard to hear, but if you do not fit in items in your closet because you plan to lose weight or have a fear of gaining any weight back, these clothes have to be moved somewhere else too. I get it, 100%. I do not want to take away the struggles so many of us face with weight and clothing.

But remember, today is about today. WHERE YOU ARE NOW. Let's give that person a chance to feel good today. Instead of worrying or focusing on who you were yesterday, or what you might look like tomorrow. Today is the day for you.

Please move all of these items to a box or bin labeled "NOT TODAY"... Maybe tomorrow, and that's ok. But NOT TODAY.

I think you will quickly uncover that you really only have a handful of clothes that you regularly wear. Now you can ask the "good stuff" questions: Do my clothes represent who I am today? Do they align with the future goals and dreams I have for myself? Do they help me live and dress on purpose? Do they make me *happy*? Or are they just seat fillers?

A *Happy Closet* helps bring happiness into your life. You can't be happy all the time, but you can at least feel *happy* in your clothes.

Lindsey's Tips
BE PICKY ABOUT YOUR HAPPY

I was nearly done writing this book and I was noticing how much I learned in the process. I could actually feel myself and my closet getting "happier" with each chapter I wrote. Here are some things I found out:

- » I only like myself in v-neck t-shirts and sweaters.
- » I only like crew-neck sweatshirts if they have hoods or are cropped styles.
- » I only like myself in wide leg jeans, so it was time to say goodbye to the skinny or slim fit. I just don't feel as sexy when I wear those styles. I accept this and move on.
- » I really like a great handbag. So this is where I choose to invest a great portion of my budget each season or once a year.
- » I only need two new shoe styles each year. Any more than that, and they don't get the wear I would want them to. (This does not include sneakers, which are practically a weekly addition for me, LOL)
- » I needed more date or dinner options. My whole wardrobe was dedicated to work.
- » It's important to have items in my closets for events that haven't happened yet. Spontaneity is a gift of life, and I want to be prepared for it!

My last realization: If you don't have anywhere to wear your clothes and that is your sole reason for not buying anything, then you need to plan more places to go. To put it bluntly, you need to get out and experience life. Make plans to see the people that bring you joy, make plans to experience this gorgeous world, make memories in your clothing by living your life. It's a double win—you get to wear beautiful clothes and make magical memories.

DAY 4

STOP DISAPPEARING

It's about to get real up in here. So grab your sparring gloves and prepare for battle…

Oh the glorious mystery of the color black. Oh the wondrous way wearing black makes us feel. So easy, so chic, so consistent, so… lazy. Yes, I said it. Lazy.

Ok, don't put the book down. Don't turn on me. Hear me out. I do believe that black has a place in your closet. I do believe it has its moment. But I firmly believe it should serve as the understudy, not the lead in your show.

I once read that black absorbs all the colors of the visible spectrum, and reflects none of them to the eyes. Do you know what this means? It means when you wear all black, from head to toe, essentially you're disappearing.

Wearing all black conveys to the world that you want to be absorbed by everything that's around you, rather than show up as the vibrant human being that you are. It is time to take a stand against wearing a color that has no identity.

Choosing to wear black every day, all the time, because you don't want to be seen, don't have the time to care about being seen, or even worse, feel like you don't deserve to be seen, literally breaks my heart.

For some of us, we don't even know what *feeling seen* means or how to wear anything but clothing that helps us disappear.

The color black in our wardrobe has taken over our lives. It has become a security blanket for any sense of style or effort to try new things, and an easy way to hide ourselves.

You might say, "I am just running around today. This plain black outfit and leggings is what makes me feel good. Obvi."

BUT DOES IT? Or does it feel like an excuse to get out the door and pray you don't run into anyone you know?

What if you decided to tell yourself another story? What if feeling good meant feeling alive? Inspired? Embodying the moment? Being present? We all talk so much about being present. We do yoga, we meditate, and go on long walks always searching for our "presence."

Being present means living and staying in the moment right now, and it includes YOU and how you show up in the world.

You are the main event. You are the story of your life. Wouldn't it feel good to enjoy the full scope of your life and how dang gorgeous you are? This means being excited to bump into someone when you are *just* running errands. If you are celebrating, show up as the celebration, not dressed for a funeral. Wear the joyous outfit that honors the moment. Do this for yourself. The value of this present moment and

YOU are worth the effort.

Today, we shall mourn the color black as it exists in our lives. We have subscribed to this notion for too long.

Coming Out of the Dark

Growing up in Las Vegas—where the sun shines an average of 310 days a year—the different weather seasons sort of blend together. It mostly feels either really hot or pretty cold, no in between. There is no real need for heavy coats or sweaters. There are really only two seasons of transition: April in the spring and October in the fall. Nearly every Halloween, the temperature would drop and we would spend the night running through the neighborhoods, ill-prepared for the chill in the air, but too excited and high on sugar to care.

Then in April, on Easter/Passover weekend, it seemed to (un)officially become the time to bust out the bright colors and embrace the expected hot summer ahead. There are no "fashion rules" in Vegas, like not wearing white after Labor Day. But something about these holidays seemed to signal it was time to show off the dazzling shades of spring's finest hues.

As I dressed for these occasions, year after year, I would always put on something lively that morning. The day seemed to mark a change in the air, an opportunity for a new beginning, starting with my wardrobe choice.

At Sunday brunch one year, I looked around the room and noticed that no one was wearing black. I spotted the occasional black accessory, but it really appeared that the attendees all got the (unsent) memo to leave their little black dress at home. I couldn't help but wonder:

WHY? What about this day, this change of the seasons, created a passion for color?

The sentiment of spring's rebirth and all the colors in full bloom represent life, change, and evolution. The world comes alive (allergies and all) with the colors of spring. The bold shades and complex tones that surround us are a reminder of the beauty in this world and all that is possible.

Color makes us feel alive. It brings out the light in our eyes, the vibrancy of our energy. It allows us to feel seen.

I want you to be seen AND to see all that's possible for you. I want to see yourself come alive, and vividly represent the voice that was put here to change the world. YOURS.

It's not to say you can't do this while wearing black. Black is powerful, all on its own. It represents fierceness. It says, "Don't mess with me."

But not when you wear it every day. That's when it says, "Don't look at me."

The way we live in black yoga pants, dark shapeless sheath dresses, and worn-out, black-faded-to-gray sweaters are NOT the black that Coco Chanel envisioned when she changed the world with the idea that women COULD and SHOULD wear black.

How are you choosing to wear black? Are you choosing it to be glamorous, seductive, and sexy? Or are you choosing it to hide?

Notice how often you turn to black clothing when you want the easy way out. Are you wearing it because you love it? Or because you love to hide behind it?

• Styling Stories •
NO BLACK CLOTHING (ON PURPOSE)

One year on Mother's Day, my client sent me a photo of herself in front of a beautiful rose bush. She was wearing a vibrant light green jumpsuit, and had a huge smile on her face. In the text, she wrote: "Look Lindsey, no black clothes today!" I cheered for her because I knew she did that on purpose.

When she sent me this message, I had recently started emphasizing the "no black clothing, on purpose" sentiment to my styling clients. I was using our appointments to show them ways to incorporate neutrals and empowering solid colors as a way to elevate their life and style. I would joke (but not really) that no black attire was to be purchased in a wardrobing session. I could see by the sparkle in their eyes that they loved this little game we were playing. Asking themselves with each new color-enhancing piece they tried on, "How can I live my life differently than I had before?"

It was like they had received a permission slip to release the dark cloak they had repeatedly been wearing all these years. I was saying to them, "You CAN wear color," and they were responding, "Show me the way, girl."

When I started on this journey myself, I would notice my thoughts as I skimmed my closet each morning. I usually left myself about 30 seconds to get dressed each day. So the obvious choices were the things that were easy, safe, and fairly systematic for me.

I would reach for my typical black turtleneck or long dress, nearly every day. It was all I knew how to do. I didn't have the mental capacity to understand how wearing all black was also a metaphor and pattern for many areas of my life. I was showing up halfway at work and in my relationships as well.

I wanted to quit playing small. I wanted to follow my dream of writing a book, starting a business, being there more for my daughter. I wanted more. I wanted to show up MORE. I didn't want to disappear any longer.

I made the choice to allot myself more than half a minute to find my outfit for the day. I started with five minutes, to be honest. With the extra "whopping" four minutes and 30 seconds, I had time to notice where my thoughts were drifting as I scanned my closet. I started to understand the energy as I reached for that same, monotonous, dreary outfit. I wanted to rise above that feeling.

I saw what I had become accustomed to. I was inauthentically drifting through my day, dressed like a stagehand, in all black. Seemingly working in the background of someone else's life.

I was ready to be the lead in my own show.

There were many days I could hear my *UnHappy Closet* talking to me, saying, "No one cares what you look like, so just wear this old black top." "No one is looking at you. Wear it." "You feel ugly today. Wear it."

Ya umm, no thank you. I began by reaching for anything that wasn't black, or wasn't in my normal rotation. That's how I started the new habit. I eliminated one thing that I felt could possibly be holding me back. I needed it to be one step at a time. The change didn't happen overnight, but I was certainly on my yellow brick road to figuring it out. I did not like "hearing" my closet telling me what to do. I wanted to find the "wizard" within myself, on my own journey towards courage and confidence.

I was practicing the activities as I was writing this book. I used tools from Day 2 to gain inspiration. Whenever I saw a neutral, non-black look on Instagram, I saved it. Over the season, I added those inspo pieces to my closet, within my budget. Thanks to my Insta Influencer (of my own life) Dream Board (from Day 2) of the book, I had a better idea of what I was looking for.

I focused on purchasing key pieces, in colors I could manage, and felt simple to throw on.

This included:

- » Two to three lightweight sweaters
- » Two V-neck T-shirts
- » Two blouses with simple patterns that I could dress up or down
- » Pleather pants in grays and browns. These can be easily paired with a great T-shirt and blazer, or a beautiful blouse for evening.
- » Two great jeans: One dressier pair that I could wear for a night out with the gals, and another pair that made me feel both comfortable and cool at the same time.
- » Two jackets: A blazer style to go over everything from jeans to a dress, and a leather jacket that was comfortable enough to wear all day. It could not be stiff or too tight. This is an absolute staple in any wardrobe.

I began to see new things about myself:

- » I noticed how pretty I looked in pink (don't we all?)
- » I noticed how my skin lit up in certain shades of brown with the right undertones. Shocking! Brown had been a color I had stayed away from my whole life. When I decided to give it a chance, I realized there were many shades of brown/neutral that actually looked pretty freakin' fabulous on me.
- » I noticed how wonderful it felt to care, really care, about showing up in the world, full of energy and life.

Dressing with colorful intention made me feel like I was giving the day my best effort, from the early morning on.

And that's why we are here today, to come out of the dark.

TRY THIS ON...
BLACK IS THE NEW BLACK

Today you are to wear only black clothing. And I mean head to toe. Black pants, black shirt, black shoes, black bag. Black underwear if you want.

The practice today is this: Notice how dressing in all black clothes makes you feel. How does it feel to wear clothes that, by definition, are meant to help you disappear?

At the end of the day, ask yourself these questions:

- » Did your all-black outfit make you feel confident today?
- » Did you feel vibrant, full of energy and excitement?

- » Were you excited to see people today?
- » Did you shy away from seeing anyone because of how you were dressed?
- » Did you notice how many people around you were also in all black today? Did you view them in a different way after noticing this?

◎ WHAT IT MEANS TO BE SEEN

As your stylist, I want you to know that recognizing how you feel today might bring up too many emotions to vocalize or fully understand. You may have spent years in this uniform, living in the shadows, because showing yourself seemed far too difficult. You may not even remember when this started. Or perhaps you can remember the exact situation that sent you here. It can be hard to live life with people *seeing* us. It makes us totally vulnerable and possibly more susceptible to judgment.

I ask you this: Who needs to worry about the judgment of other people when we are already being so hard on ourselves? We have created our own story before we have given the outside world a chance to read the book, truly as it's been written.

For many of you, today will represent coming out of the dark. You are not alone. Now, from each day forward, you will have the tools to face this.

On the days you have the urge to wear all black, and you choose not to, *on purpose*, you are growing. Your light is certain to become brighter, beaming as unexpected doors open for you.

My friend, it's time to shimmy and shine into the world.

DAY 5

BOLDLY FILL THE UNIVERSE

Color creates vibrancy in our lives, no matter how we decide to wear it. From lipsticks and eyeshadows, to self-tanner and nail polish. We embellish ourselves with color as a way of saying, "I'm here baby. I deserve to take up space in the world." Wearing dynamic hues, or powerful, neutral clothing is an opportunity to allow your personality and identity to shine.

One of the first things we enjoy as children is color, and deciding which is our favorite. Then we declare it to the world and beg to wear it all the time!

But as we get older, we tend to stop wanting to stand out as the cute girl dressed in all pink or purple. We begin to dim our light, out of fear of being "too much" or "too loud."

At three years old, you don't hear many kids saying, "My favorite color is black." A room full of preschoolers would be shouting, "Pink, yellow, blue, red, orange, purple!" They want you to know which color is theirs, and they are so proud of it.

So when did we lose that lust for color? When did black become our fave? And, if it's not our fave, why do we wear it so freakin' much?

That was a phenomenon we addressed on Day 4.

We began the conversation of how we "sink" into our clothes. Hiding between the fibers that cover the deepest parts of our insecurity. Most days are filled with just getting by, no time to actually engage in the world. WE ARE BUSY. We are on the go, go, go until the sun goes down and we do it all over again when the sun comes up.

I see it daily as I walk the streets of New York. The panic in people's eyes as they rush to get to where they need to be, dressed haphazardly, just happy to have made it out the door. Survival and black spandex are the most cherished resources for us most days.

Now, I am asking you to stop and notice. I'd like you to take a moment to pause with me, and ask yourself:

When was the last time you allowed yourself to live out loud? How often have you opted for the bolder choice over the darker one?

Maybe you are telling yourself that you just happen to like black. Maybe you are saying that color isn't your thing.

Defining a color palette that you love, be it rich pinks and blues, or dreamy whites and yummy creams, is POWER. Think of how it would feel to highlight the glorious tones of your skin, or choose to wear something that represents a bolder expression of who you are. It says to the world, "What I have to say matters." Without even having to say a word.

When you wear things out of habit or sheer routine, you are not dressing with purpose. We get in the routine of waking up, getting dressed, going to work, coming home, eating dinner, going to bed... and repeat. That's the rut we can all easily fall into.

When you see movies or read books where people make abrupt changes and throw caution to the wind, they are lifting themselves out of their rut. But in real life, we can't just throw our lives away when we all of a sudden wake up and are totally bored of our routine.

What if, instead, you found small ways to fill your soul, your cup, and your heart on a daily basis. This could help stop patterns or habits before they get out of hand, hence the feeling that there is no other option than to leave it all behind. The way we dress can be one of these motivating lifelines.

Let's think about where you start and end your day.

You begin your morning with the choice of how to show up today by deciding what to wear. You end your day by coming home and anxiously tearing off your clothes to get comfy—hating or loving each piece as you toss it in the laundry basket. Thinking about how you can't wait for the day to be over.

Maybe you say, as you toss your jeans into the bin, "I am never wearing these again. I hated them today." Yet, when they are clean, you will. Because they are safe and habitual, which is a lot easier than bold and trailblazing.

Wouldn't it be lovely to take off your outfit and say, "I was so cute today. Everyone loved this shirt!" and then reflect on all the good and wondrous things you experienced in the last eight hours?

Our energy rolls into more energy. The more positive, or the

more negative. **The decision as to which way to go is up to you.**

I understand that you may not be ready to totally fill the universe just yet. What I dream for you is that you uncover an understanding of what purposefully taking up more space could feel like. Each day is meant to help you further observe how you show up for yourself. Start proving to yourself that even on your laziest day, you can feel 15% better than you have ever looked and felt in years, or possibly ever.

• Styling Stories •
BLAIRE IN COLOR

I started working with a client who didn't believe she could wear anything but black or really dark colors. I mean, she was a New Yorker, I get it. When she started the appointment with me, her hesitation was palpable. "This is who I am," she exclaimed. She had not had the time to think of anything else, she was too busy managing her job, her family, all things "life."

Prior to any appointment with a new client, I ask them to send me a recent photo of themselves. You'd be surprised how many women do not have a recent photo. Even with the popularity of social media, most women say, "I don't have one," or "Let me look, I'm not sure I have."

What does that tell you?

This client sent me a photo and told me it was a picture of herself in an outfit she really liked that she wore three years ago. I stopped her and said, "The last photo you have of yourself in an outfit you liked was three years ago?" She simply said, "Yes."

The picture she sent me was her in all black, with a white shirt barely poking out underneath the blazer. On the bottom she donned a slim, narrow-fitting jean. I couldn't wait to help her. I couldn't wait to watch her come alive among the perfectly suited colors I planned to pull for her.

As I prepped for her appointment, I quickly walked past the shocking pinks that I would have grabbed for the previous client. I skipped over the browny colored creams that would be too nude for her pale skin.

Instead, I picked up the pinky neutrals that were the right tones for her hair color. The shades of green to highlight her eyes. I skipped any black, and opted for variations of navy and blues with chic silhouettes.

This is how I shop for all my clients. I wander the floors of the store, perfectly curating exactly what is best for the woman in front of me. It's such a special and rare feeling to know that someone did all this, just for you. The sole purpose of the styling appointment is for you to feel your best and build a *Happy Closet* for yourself. It's awesome to see a client's expression when they walk into a room JUST FOR THEM!

That day in the fitting room, I watched Blaire come to life in her colors. I saw something awaken in her that she hadn't thought was possible, at least not in recent years. She was absolutely hesitant at first. We had to ease into this transition. First starting with pieces I knew were in her comfort zone, and then mixing in the items that pushed her outside the box she had believed she belonged in.

The more she tried, the more she began to understand the assignment.

Blaire left with a handful of items that she would have never tried if we hadn't spent that time together. Mostly because she didn't even know how to find clothing she never knew she was looking for!

We don't know what we don't know. We are drawn to the same things over and over, in so many aspects of life. Learning how to style ourselves in a new way is hard. It's much easier to feel safe than to be seen. But when you choose to do this for yourself, it's magic.

The best text messages I receive are from clients in the days that follow our appointment. "Lindsey, I wore my new shirt today. I felt so good. Even my daughter told me I looked pretty. Shocking for a 13-year-old to say. I love the color so much. Thank you." Or "Lindsey, I felt so good last night. I had the best time. I know it had a lot to do with how cute I felt in my outfit. Thank you."

Wouldn't it be fun for you to send me a text like that? I look forward to it.

TRY THIS ON...
COLOR OUTSIDE THE LINES

Now, raise your hand if you guessed what the activity was going to be today. Good job. You guessed it.

Today you are to wear no black clothing. Today you will live in color.

You can wear whatever color you have in your closet. White is a color, so is pink, and pattern, anything that is not 75% black.

Your shirt should be a shade that makes you smile, or if nothing else, brings out the tones of your hair or eyes. If you only have black pants, ask yourself why you have limited yourself to only one way to express yourself each day.

Wear as much color as your current wardrobe allows. Maybe it's a lot to ask you to do this, because it has been so long since your outfit helped tell your story. If this is the case, wear a bright pink lip, a shirt with a fun pattern, or a dress that you have been itching for an excuse to put on for a while. The point is, wear something different than you normally would, and do it IN COLOR!

Also, in case you haven't picked up on this—no black yoga pants today either.

At the end of today, I encourage you to answer these questions in your journal or in the notes section of your phone:

- » How did you feel at the end of the day?
- » Did you notice what the intention of showing up in color felt like?
- » At what point, if any, did you feel out of place in your colorful outfit?
- » Did something special or memorable happen today?
- » At the end of the day, how did you feel taking your outfit off?
- » What unexpected story or surprise happened in your outfit?
- » Did you feel like MORE today?

◊ MORE IS MORE

Today is a practice in truly beginning to notice your choices. Are you struggling with doing the activities or even the sheer idea of them?

Are you coming up with excuses about why this book is stupid and no one should tell you how to dress? Are you feeling like you are enough as you are, and none of this is relatable?

I mean, same. I am enough, as I am.

But I do love seeing how I can evolve. My bedside table is filled with books on how to evolve, who I can become, and how to improve in various aspects of my life. I love it all. Give me all the info I can to make this one life of mine a tiny bit MORE meaningful.

Sometimes I do need to grant myself permission to take up MORE space, and that's ok. Reading books or listening to great podcasts helps me identify who I am, and it helps me step into my MORE with confidence. When I am connected to my purpose, when I show up as my true self in hot pink, I am MORE.

MORE loving to my friends.

MORE in tune with my career.

MORE dedicated to the planet and being a good person.

MORE confident in the message I want to convey to the world.

I want this for you. I want you to be MORE. I want you to be the MOST. You are worthy of that. There is no story greater than the one you are here to tell.

I want you to uncover the part of you that has more to offer. As much as you may not like to be told what to do, or want to realize that the clothes you wear matter. I am asking you to put that part of you aside, just for the next few days.

I am excited for you to notice how you walk into a room and own that entrance. I am thrilled for you to understand you are MORE—more confident, more persuasive, more purposeful.

We are magnets to change and attracted to color. We are naturally drawn to those that express themselves boldly, with confidence and courage. When you show up in a vibrant way online or in real life, you are living at a high vibration of greatness, which is in line with the intention of the magnificent world around you.

The world lives in color, and that's what makes us love it. When the sun shines, we shine. We would literally die without it. Animals use color to show courage and to protect themselves. Peacocks expand their brilliant feathers to attract their mates and intimidate their predators. We, as a collective, speak in color.

We travel the planet to see the deepest blue oceans, mountains of rich earthy tones that stand surrounded by white puffy clouds. We travel for hours to walk on soft sand beaches and look out at the turquoise sea we long to splash in. The open sky calls to us. The green meadows invite us to dance among the wildflowers of purple, pink and yellow.

The world is alive with color, and we would never dare ask it to be anything other than the perfect magnificence it is.

You are worthy of expecting this very same thing for yourself.

Lindsey's Tips
UNSOLICITED ADVICE AT THE HALFWAY POINT

There is a difference between a HABIT, a UNIFORM, and a continuous STYLE EVOLUTION.

When you have a uniform, you might initially wear that uniform and enjoy how cool it makes you feel. You enjoy the simplicity and streamlined ease of your cool capsule wardrobe. It is fabulous to feel complete and put together.

The difference is when you begin to wear the uniform out of habit and not because it's part of your *"chic minimalist"* vibe. This is when it stops being inspiring.

When it feels like you are wearing it because you don't know how to wear anything else. It's time to change.

The foundation of your style evolution is the willingness to change.

In order to change, you have to be willing to try new things. If you say "NO" to what it feels like to live and dress differently, then you will continue to see the same results, in all aspects of your life.

Being inspired by the world around you and other people is part of the joy of life. Even if you tried to copy their style exactly, it would still never be the same.

Your own voice and energy make you authentic. You are undeniably and unequivocally YOU. Step into that space.

DAY 6

THANKS FOR THE MEMORIES

Confident decision-making (for myself) has never been my strong suit. Isn't that a funny play on words?

Anyway, I had dreamed about moving to New York City since I was fourteen years old, but it took me a while to get there. My friends used to say that if indecision could take over someone's body, it had taken over mine. It was true. I am a Libra and making a decision is pretty brutal for me. But I knew I always wanted to live in the Big Apple.

I didn't know how I would do it, but the longing was a terrible ache in my bones. I used to watch TV shows set in New York City, with characters living among the skyscrapers and I would be so jealous of them... silly, I know. But my life was in Las Vegas. I was comfortable there, and at the top of my career game. There was too much at stake to leave.

I was 34 when I finally did it.

I moved across the country, and just started over. I sold everything I owned and moved into a studio apartment on the Upper West Side of Manhattan. I sold hundreds of things, from my shoes, to my furniture, and even my car.

I also decided to only bring along the clothing that served the new New York version of me. Plus, the closet in my apartment was pretty small. I even had to put my shoes in my kitchen pantry, FOR REAL! I needed to be picky. It was a great exercise in finding out who I really was, on all levels. I couldn't believe I was capable of doing any of it, but I did.

Two weeks after I arrived, I was ready to hit the ground running as a New York stylist. On my first day of work at luxury department store Bergdorf Goodman, I wore the most incredible cashmere turtleneck and stunning silk taffeta, high-waisted skirt. I was for sure channeling Audrey Hepburn in *Breakfast at Tiffany's*.

It was New York, New Me. I felt powerful. I felt polished. I was ready to start my next chapter.

There was a sleet/snowstorm that morning on my way into work, but I was unstoppable. I even had the courage to ask a stranger to share a cab with me, when we both tried to hop in one at the same time. We were two women on a mission. I thought, "Why fight when we're both headed in the same direction?" By the way, this has never happened to me again since that day—Ha!

I walked across 5th Avenue and into the gold revolving doors of Bergdorf's like I owned the place.

Who was I to have all this confidence? I was a West Coast girl who knew nothing about the big city. But I looked the part, and I had gotten myself this far. I wasn't backing down now.

The memory of that wild February morning lives on so clearly in my mind. The very thought of it brings me so much joy—that vision of a courageous me in that fabulously chic "Audrey" skirt. I am so grateful for the power it gave me that morning. It helped me show up on purpose, and start my new life, on my terms.

Can you think of an outfit that has given you great memories?

What We Remember

Our daily life and core memories are created in the clothes we are wearing, yet we barely consider this as we get dressed each day. Our clothes are with us through it all. On the days we bid farewell and fly away from our homes and families, they are there. They live in the photo albums and picture frames on our walls. We diligently pack them as we travel the world on vacation. They are part of our journey.

You create powerful memories in the wardrobe you choose. Memories that, good or bad, can last a lifetime. We are thankful for the funny nights with our girlfriends, where you laughed till 2 AM. We are thankful for the cozy onesie we brought our child home from the hospital in, and the stretch pants that got you through your postpartum days.

We are taught to be thankful AND to say thank you for many things. When someone holds the door open, thank you. When we receive a gift, whether we want it or not, thank you. We say thank you all day long.

But rarely do we say thank you for the sweater that keeps us warm, the bathing suit that allows us to joyfully bask in the ocean waves, or the awesome way we looked in that hot pink dress on our 21st birthday.

What if we had the same gratitude for our clothing as we do for the memories we create while wearing them?

In the past, I have taken my clothes for granted. Thinking of them as something I merely throw on to get out the door.

In reality, our clothes speak for us before we even have a chance. They are part of our brand. They can be the secret to our success.

When you understand what it means to dress on purpose, we begin to see the power we have in our clothing, and the impact it has had on our lives.

Even if today you may not have a closet or wardrobe that you love, there were times in your life that you fondly remember the way you dressed and felt really special in an outfit you wore. Maybe it was your wedding day, your first day at a new job, a first date, or the day you got engaged. There is some memory in there that is better because of what you were wearing.

• Styling Stories •
NINA'S LAST-MINUTE TRIP

One of my clients, Nina, married for the second time in her early 50s. She met the love of her life in an unexpected way and certainly remembers exactly what she was wearing on their first date. Now they have been married for a few years. One Thursday morning her husband sent her a text message telling her to pack her bags and prepare for a romantic weekend away, just the two of them.

(When you are spontaneously in love at 50, you just go with it. Wherever the road may lead, you are up for the adventure. That is something you should never grow out of or think you aren't worthy of experiencing.)

Nina had a very short amount of time to pack and prep for this trip, and she was given little guidance on what to bring. She did know that the trip included a car ride, a fancy dinner, and a fun walking-around day to dress for.

In that moment, Nina was extra appreciative of her *Happy Closet*, knowing she could quickly grab the items that would ensure she exuded confidence that weekend. By the time Nina got to the hotel, she couldn't wait to get dressed for dinner. She had packed her favorite low-cut, pale blue top and skintight leather pants. It was the top she wore when her husband had proposed to her.

She knew it would bring an instant level of desire to the evening. Nina felt so sexy. Not only because she felt desired by her husband, but because she knew she looked good. The weekend was a major success, and Nina was dazzling. The memories from that trip live on in her mind and in her closet, each time she sees that blue top.

BUT, before we pat ourselves on the back and move on, let's consider another way this story *could* have gone. Think Gwyneth Paltrow's character in the movie *Sliding Doors*.

Let's rewind... Nina gets the text from her husband to be packed and ready for this seductive trip, ASAP. Nina then furiously starts looking through her closet for something to pack. Imagine a scene where clothes are flying through the air and piling up on the bed faster than the speed of light.

"Hate this, doesn't fit, so ugly, why do I still have this, boring, worn a million times, UGH!"

These are all things Nina said to herself and to her *UnHappy Closet* as she was trying to pack. First, Nina thought about canceling. How annoying of her husband to expect her to be packed and ready for a trip on THIS short notice!!

She had the perfect collection of cozy sets and yoga pants ready for a workout retreat; couldn't he just have planned that! But she knew it was actually pretty cute of him to plan this. It wasn't his fault that she had nothing to wear.

Sigh, she was annoyed at herself but she didn't have much time to sulk. The clock was ticking.

Nina tossed her typical black dress, black leggings, gray T-shirt and jean jacket in her bag. She headed out the door and hopped in the car, still annoyed but mostly at herself.

That night at the fabulous dinner, all Nina could think about was how underdressed and uncomfortable she felt. The next day, she didn't feel like taking any pictures either.

Her somber outfit didn't match the energy of the cute, quaint town they were visiting, *or* the magic of the moment her husband had created.

She knew it was silly, but she wished she had taken the time to create a wardrobe that was as fulfilling as the rest of her life. She wanted to feel as confident on the outside, as her husband and this moment had made her feel on the inside.

In this scenario, Nina may look back on this weekend with a bit of sadness.

Nina was thankful for her husband, and thankful for the thoughtful surprise, but she certainly wasn't thankful for the dreary clothes that made her feel meh. Her life was so much more than *meh*.

Don't be this Nina.

Be the Nina with a *Happy Closet*, super thankful for the effortless ability to show up anywhere, at the drop of a hat, with confidence.

TRY THIS ON...
DEAR CLOSET, THANK YOU.

As you reflect back on your life, think about the special days and the outfits you were wearing.

Was the day fantastic because you loved the way you looked, or did you love the way you looked, so the day was fantastic?

Do you remember feeling really fab in a few things you have worn over the years? What made you feel that way? Did you love the color? Did you love the comfort it gave you? The power you felt you had over the room?

Today you are going to say thank you for the clothing you have worn—from when you were little, through all the eras of your life.

You will say thank you for the seemingly mundane items, like your socks. Then you will remember your favorite shoes, the ones you splurged on and felt like Sarah Jessica Parker wearing. Then move on to the big fish, the big memories and what you wore that day. You can relish in your rehearsal dinner outfit, your farewell party dresses, or simply your most favorite jeans and shirts. The ones that seem to give you superpowers.

This is your moment to brag about yourself and how great you looked that day, how much fun you had that night, and how you were on top of the world in that dress.

Think about all the magical ways your clothing has played a part in your daily life and your most memorable activities. Be impressed with what you have done and how you felt doing it. What did you wear that day? What outfit will you never forget?

Look back on certain experiences in your life and the clothing you wore to the occasions. Ask yourself these questions, and write down the answers in your journal:

- » What was a day in your life when you felt beautiful in your clothing?
- » What were you wearing, what were you doing, and who were you with?
- » How did it make you feel to know you really LIKED the way you looked?
- » Do you especially enjoy those memories today? Why?

On the Flip Side...

- » What was an occasion that you felt uncomfortable the whole day or night because you DIDN'T like the way you looked or felt?
- » What was it about that day? Did you not give yourself enough time to get dressed or pick the look? Did you not try the outfit

on and it no longer fit you or your style anymore?

» Did you keep the uninspired or uncomfortable item, even though you knew it no longer served you?

If your answer keeps coming back to your weight, or because you were thinner, let's pause. If you think it's because you were younger and more beautiful, then you are missing the significance of this message. You can have that same feeling, that same energy, at any age and size. You have to choose YOU, and the world will meet you with applause.

Before you end this day, take a moment to say thank you for never having to worry if you would have socks to wear or a warm coat in the winter. Find gratitude for all the amazing experiences you have enjoyed in your clothing, and all the miracles you have experienced wearing them. (Insert clapping here.)

◎ OPPORTUNITIES AHEAD

Back to Nina (again). The truth is you don't always get six months to plan the perfect dress or outfit. You don't always get an invite two weeks before an event to help plan how you will show up that night. Life is spontaneous. Some of the best nights are the ones you never saw coming. Having a *Happy Closet*, and a wardrobe that matches your endless possibilities, opens up the opportunity for life to inspire you, photograph you, and elevate you—any random day of the week.

What you wear has helped shape many of the most special occasions in your life. There is a reason you want your wedding dress to be perfect on your wedding day, or that you plan the prettiest outfit for your birthday or graduation.

We are all aware of how our clothing makes us feel on special occasions. So why do we put so little effort into all the days in between?

Ask yourself, do you live in black leggings and old shirts because you feel that, most likely, today really isn't that important? Perhaps you are spending too much of your life waiting for that surprise trip or seductive text to dress with purpose. Now ask yourself this: WHY WAIT? You are worthy of this today.

DAY 7

A MORE POWERFUL VERSION OF YOU

In my twenties, as I started to make more money, I began to buy a few expensive or special pieces of clothing and accessories. I noticed that I was always "saving" them.

If I bought a pair of jeans, or a T-shirt that I was "obsessed" with, I would wait and wait until the perfect moment to wear it. Perhaps I was afraid of ruining it, or worried that my cute look would be wasted on a pointless day. IDK!

I think it's safe to say that we all have that piece (or pieces) of clothing in our closet that we "conserve." We bought it because it felt like a special investment or maybe we splurged on it. For whatever reason, this item holds a piece of your heart that often makes it a "struggle" to wear.

So now, it sits, like a shrine in your closet, patiently waiting for its day in the sun.

I see this all the time with my clients. **We buy things to "save" them. We wait to wear things. We wait and wait.** Sometimes we do get that perfect moment. Sometimes we miss out on it too.

Although no client is the same, I do notice that the women who choose to wear their new clothes right away tend to find more value in their experience with me. When they wear their new outfit that weekend or that month, they see and feel the results immediately.

When you shift, the world notices right away.

When I receive messages from clients, bright and early on Monday morning, I am so inspired. I love hearing the rundown on the fabness of their weekend. I love that they have taken their new purposeful dressing by the "horns" and "ain't no one going to hold them back."

They are stepping into the new version of themselves right away. This leaves more space for greatness to come, and faster.

• Styling Stories •
YOU NEVER KNOW WHERE YOUR CLOTHES WILL TAKE YOU

David, a young professional, was navigating his career. He was at a crossroads, looking for the path he truly wanted to take, versus the route he was currently on.

David had been to many of my speaking engagements. After a few times, he started to understand what it meant to "dress on purpose." Also, he loved the concept I spoke about, teaching my clients how to dress for the next version of themselves.

He began to embrace my tips on what it means *to "dress today for the life you want tomorrow."* This is a message I weave into all my fashion presentations and styling appointments. It's a powerful concept, whether you are a business professional or anyone looking to expand your future.

David decided to buy a few new things at a time I like to call "Spring Fever." It's when the sun decides to start shining in early spring and all of a sudden you have this realization that you have nothing to wear and need all new clothes.

As David browsed online, attempting to rehabilitate his current shopping ailments, he saw the fork in the road I had so frequently spoken of at my fashion events.

He started to "add to cart" all his usuals: the khaki pants to replace last year's khaki pants; a new blue button down since his current shirt had been over dry-cleaned; the same cotton-blend blazer he had been wearing since grad school. Then he stopped.

He remembered that all-cream look he had seen on a movie character recently. He wasn't sure he could rock it, but you know what? He was willing to try.

David started searching the shopping site differently. He filtered out his usual blues and grays, and pivoted towards creams and chic neutrals. He felt it. He wasn't willing to take the easy road this time. He was ready to see if purposeful dressing could make a difference in his life.

Departing from his usual routine, he chose:

» Elevated, dressy polos instead of stiff button-down shirts

- » A blazer with texture and an understated collar
- » A few pairs of luxurious denim jeans
- » A chic cream pant
- » Brown leather sneakers
- » A beautifully designed sock to slightly poke out from his pants and inspire elegance

As he checked out, he felt like the next version of himself already. David made a choice at that moment. He decided that the routine was not going to win again.

A few days later, his new clothes arrived. He decided to have a new headshot taken for his LinkedIn profile. David wasn't sure what it meant. He wasn't even looking for a new job. But he thought it was worth putting this new, updated version of himself out there, just because.

Within three days, he received a call from one of the top PR firms in the world. They wanted him. They told him his profile and bio were perfect for the role they were looking to fill.

It all happened so fast and so easily. Within a few short weeks, the new version of David walked into his new office, cream outfit and all.

When David and I talked about this story, he thanked me. He believed that my message was top of mind for him the night he had shopped for the clothes that catapulted him on this new adventure.

I love this story. It reminds me that if David had stalled on wearing his new clothes for too long because he was waiting for the "perfect" day, he might have missed out on this opportunity altogether.

Maybe David's new wardrobe had nothing to do with how things worked out; maybe it did. We won't ever really know. The science-backed phenomena of quantum physics and the Law of Attraction suggest that we attract "like vibrations."

When we live at a higher level, more high-level situations are attracted to us. You can be a beacon of attraction when you show up in a way that elevates you. Give yourself the chance to see if it's true.

TRY THIS ON...
TODAY'S THE PERFECT DAY

Think about where YOU are today. You have accomplished so much already. It's pretty incredible to think of everything else you can create for yourself in your purposeful wardrobe.

In this exercise, you are going to live as if today is the perfect day. The perfect day to be the next level of you. It starts right now.

When you open your closet to get dressed for the day, no matter what your plan is, you are going to wear that coveted item in your closet. The blouse you love, the jeans you adore, or the dress that makes you smile just by looking at it. Grab the first item that your eyes lock onto, and just put it on.

Perhaps today is a work day. Maybe today's practice coincides with a big meeting. Or maybe you are just staying home today. Wherever you are going, even to the grocery store, you are going to wear this item.

Notice how you feel as you walk out the door. Are you thinking of the story of the day you bought this? Are you worried how people will look at you? Does it just feel like any old outfit, or does something about it make you feel special? Even in some small way?

I don't suggest a gown or overly dressy cocktail outfit. Unless of course, you are going to a cocktail party. Then wear it, girl!

Today, wear something in your closet that you have been saving for the perfect situation. Because today IS perfect.

Now ask yourself...

- » How did you feel about grabbing it?
- » Did it make you uncomfortable to wear something so precious or special to you?
- » Was your day worthy of this outfit? Are you?
- » Can you think of another coveted piece to make a part of your usual dressing routine?
- » What was one great thing that happened today? Savor the feeling of it, and soon you'll fondly recall the memory of it. This is how confidence is built—slowly, and over time.

◎ THIS DAY TESTED ME

When I did this practice, I chose to wear a beautiful and bold blouse I had bought a few months back. I didn't wear it for many months because I didn't want to "waste" it. I begrudgingly grabbed the blouse and forced "today to be the day." When I looked at myself in the mirror throughout the day, I felt proud.

Proud that I made the decision to wear it. Grateful that I could afford such a beautiful blouse. Powerful for who I was.

Well, that morning didn't go as smoothly as I had hoped. I received terrible news of an unexpected home expense that nearly crushed my soul. I wanted to cry and scream, "NOOOOO! Not on the day I finally decided to wear my new top!"

Knowing I was writing this book and practicing living and dressing on purpose, I decided to reframe this painful and frustrating situation. I decided that I would not let this stunning shirt be marked by the pain of this day.

I forced myself to see the good in every other thing that came my way. I called a friend I could vent to (and also told her about my cute top). When she saw the pic, she oohed and ahhed. I then called three clients to generate some financial energy, and I led my team like the boss they needed me to be.

Let me tell you, bad things happen in good outfits. To be honest, I was going to get that phone call regardless of what I was wearing that day. When you take the time to center yourself as the creator of your world, you become the most powerful creator of your life. And this should be done in a great outfit.

Lindsey's Tips
DON'T TELL ME TO CHANGE

Change is such an interesting concept. When someone tells you that you have to change, it doesn't feel good. For me when someone asks me to change, all I want to say is, "Don't tell me what to do!"

It awakens a piece of me that feels *not good enough*. When we make the decision to change for ourselves, it feels empowering.

The world loves a good transformation story, be it in nature or among humans. We are fascinated with the science of caterpillars becoming butterflies, and the eerily cool concept of snakes shedding their skin. Through this process, they're making room for the new, fresh versions of themselves.

When you see your friend make major shifts, we say, "Yep, she just decided one day that she was going to change, and she did!" It's exciting to know you are capable of change, but it has to be your choice.

Dressing for the "next version of you" can be difficult. Welcoming change and finding the time to execute your new ideas can feel overwhelmingly impossible.

This is why so many of our grandiose plans fail. There seems to be barely enough time in the day to manage all our current tasks, let alone the thoughts that we push to the back of our mind for tomorrow.

As you read through this book, I hope you are beginning to

understand the parts of you that are ready to be uncovered.

Wouldn't it be exciting to actually feel change for yourself, even if at first it felt unnoticeable by others?

DAY 8

A CLOSET FULL OF COMPLIMENTS

When we see someone who is well-dressed or put together, we can often feel intimidated by it. We think to ourselves, "Why is she so overdressed?" or "If I had her body, I would dress like her too!"

Unconsciously, we are then putting ourselves down or making excuses for our own appearance. "I have no time for all the effort required to look like that!" "Well, she clearly doesn't have children to take care of!"

Whatever story we tell ourselves, it usually starts with a negative judgment about someone else, and ends with a negative thought about our own appearance or choices. Very rarely do we look at someone and say, "Wow, I love that she is wearing an outfit that is clearly much cuter than mine!"

You have been there. I have been there. When we are feeling insecure about ourselves, it feels nearly impossible to appreciate that chic person staring in our direction. Let alone give them a genuine compliment.

But as we know, everyone is fighting a silent battle we know nothing about. We all have our own story of what holds us back in life. Whether you are a size 00 or a size 20, a working woman or a stay-at-home mom. If you are financially free or tied down, we all have days that are harder than others.

• Styling Stories •
COMPLIMENTS FOR KRISTIN

Who are we when the life we planned falls apart? How do we navigate what that means for the dreams we once had?

Many clients have come to me in the darkest days of their lives. Be it fresh off a failed marriage, job loss, or other dramatic changes. I meet many women when they are re-examining what their life means to them.

Some clients are looking for cute, casual clothes, and others are looking for a rebrand. I do it all.

My styling appointments are centered around who the client wants to be, and how they want to show up.

In a styling session, as you try on clothing, you shed the various versions of your story, your past and what you thought was your future. You are naked both emotionally and physically.

Together, we work to uncover how you see yourself today, and where you want to be in the future.

Cue Kristin, a momma who was looking to pick up the pieces of her life, including what was in her closet.

Kristin had spent the last 10 years raising her daughter. She had been focused on navigating her life as a parent, someone single, and as a woman.

When Kristin started working with me, her confidence was in the red. Her husband had recently moved out. No one, in a very long time, had told her that she was beautiful or sexy. She didn't even tell herself that.

She assumed that for one to be considered sexy, the mommy pooch and c-section scar couldn't exist. She also begrudgingly accepted that her hair didn't wrap perfectly into a messy bun or that she couldn't properly contour her cheeks with makeup. She felt left behind in a world that seemed to be moving on, filled with younger, more hip versions of what she once was.

One day, I pushed Kristin to buy a dress that was totally out of her comfort zone.

Each appointment, I get one "veto." This is a chance for me to overrule the client's opinion and insist on one look that I know will change their lives. The rest, we meet somewhere in the middle.

Remember, uncovering your style identity and purposeful dressing is a muscle that needs to be toned. It's the evolution of you, built over time for great success. The first few styling sessions are usually about shedding the habits and "comfortable" pieces that have kept us safe, and welcoming new additions that allow us to shine.

Back to Kristin.

I said, "Kristin, wear this dress tomorrow and report back how many compliments you receive." I asked her to text me a check mark each time that she received some sort of compliment that day.

She pretended to fight me for a minute and then promised to send me check marks as her day progressed.

The next morning my day started with a check mark from Kristin at 9:08 AM, then another at 10:40 AM, and another at 1:18 PM. This went on until after 5:30 PM. I called Kristin for the details, eager to find out what had happened.

Some of the compliments included, "I love that color on you." "Your hair looks amazing today" (same hair as every day). "Where did you get that dress? It's so cool." "Your skin is glowing!"

And the best part was, when she looked in the mirror at the end of the day, she saw herself.

She saw her glowing skin, her pretty hair, her cool dress. She felt the intensity of the confidence rushing through her blood. She felt a purpose to herself that had indeed awakened her soul.

Dressing to be seen reminds us that we matter. That our footprint resonates with others in a way we often forget is possible. Big or small. Kristin had inspired herself that day. Who knows how many other people she motivated to toss on their own cool look the next day? The cycle is boundless.

TRY THIS ON...
NOTICE THE WORLD AROUND YOU

Today your mission is to compliment at least five people. This day is about reaching into your heart and finding ways to make sure everyone you connect with today feels absolutely stunning. In doing so, you will feel stunning too. You are going to give at least five people a closet full of compliments.

You could remark on the color of their shirt. Maybe their outfit inspired you to try a new look tomorrow. Perhaps you love the style of their jeans or the cute shoes they are wearing.

Compliment earrings, purses, patterns. Find the beauty of someone's fashion choice in as many people as you can today.

You will see joy in watching their eyes light up as you make their day with your kind words. I am sure you will also discover something new about yourself along the way.

Opening your eyes to the colorful world around you can only bring more light in your direction. You will notice what others are wearing and slowly you will see the difference a little extra effort makes in your appearance and in your energy.

Notice the joy you bring them with your genuine praise. As you spread your fashionable love today, observe how you feel about yourself. Find a quiet moment to reflect on the praise you deserve.

In a day filled with complimenting others, remember to spare a moment for yourself. Do you like the shirt you are wearing, the jeans you chose, the earrings that frame your gorgeous face?

If the answer is no, then ask yourself why you are wearing them. Why do you choose to face the world in things you don't even like?

But if you DO like what you see, give yourself some credit and a compliment. Because the first and last gesture of kindness every day should be for yourself.

❖ ARE YOU FOR REAL?

When someone compliments you, it can feel two ways... Real or fake. And to be honest, it doesn't matter either way. You probably do look really cute today, and your top is a pretty pattern. You can choose to accept that you look fab, or you can think that this person is just trying to "butter you up." Either way, your top is still cute.

A person giving a compliment can gain just as much as the person receiving it. When you give a compliment to someone else, you are taking the time to show them that you notice. You are taking a moment from your own thoughts and busyness, to tell someone that you see them. **That is the power of a compliment. I SEE YOU.**

Giving compliments increases happiness, strengthens resilience, and creates a ripple of positivity in the world around you.

DAY 9

JFDI - JUST FREAKIN' DOING IT

Elyse wanted more from her life. She wanted to be an entrepreneur, to carve an unseen path for herself. She had always followed the status quo—college, job, marriage, kids, etc. You know, the "white picket fence" story.

But she was craving more. She wanted to do something "bigger," but she was stuck. Her mind was filled with intrusive thoughts that were holding her back: "You don't even know what you are doing." "You are too old to start a business. What do you know?" "You don't have the right education or training. No one will listen to you." And the greatest dream killer, "I am an imposter. I don't really have the ability or skills to do this. Everyone else does."

Nothing can destroy a great idea more than your own thoughts.

When you experience these immobilizing feelings, overcoming them can feel impossible. Too often, we talk ourselves out of something that could be truly wonderful, if we gave it the air to breathe and space to grow.

There are a ton of self-help books, podcasts, and social media accounts dedicated solely to these very issues. But until you have felt both what it feels like to stay in these thoughts AND what it feels to move out of them, none of it feels relatable.

Elyse decided to tackle these thoughts ONE AT A TIME.

She wrote down a list of what was needed to implement her first business idea: website, social media, hire an assistant, mission statement. She started talking with friends about her fears and struggles, vocalizing what she was experiencing. Sometimes just verbalizing her thoughts gave her the answers she needed immediately. Doing one thing each day meant a slow and steady climb, but it was the way forward.

Elyse is still on her road. I can't yet tell you that this story has the ending of her being a powerful CEO or a judge on Shark Tank... YET. But I can say that Elyse is a metaphor for "Just Freakin' DO It."

What if you looked at your closet the same way? One day at a time. Thinking to yourself, "Today, I can dress on purpose. I don't know about tomorrow, but today I will allot myself the five to seven minutes needed to do this for me."

What if you started to add purposeful dressing to your to-do list? Wouldn't it feel good to check something off the list first thing in the morning that's actually super meaningful? YOU.

If you are up for this adventure and ready to squash those intrusive thoughts, I have an agenda with your name on it.

I Think We're Onto Something

Living and dressing on purpose means being purposeful in how you approach your life. Like Elyse, setting realistic expectations and doing minor things each day can help yield major results.

This is the same for your closet, and the contents of it.

If you are spending time digging through clothes you don't like, won't wear, or don't have a use for, it leaves less time for you to easily locate the things that do. DO bring out your energy, DO bring you joy, DO make your closet *Happy*. DO help you create your business, start a new career, take risks, and create change in your life.

When your closet is a sea of black or gray, everything blends together. This can make it impossible to figure out what to wear. So you just grab what you know, and throw on that top you don't really like—again. The same actions yield the same results, and we are here for *happy* and new results. NOT the same.

What items are you AVOIDING, ignoring, digging through? What are you putting off doing that is holding you back from better? Today, in your closet, let's figure it out and JUST DO IT.

Are you tired of trying on three bras in the morning until you find the one that actually fits? Or worse, are you wearing the same one over and over, continuously ignoring the pile of undergarments that you know you will never wear? Is your bathing suit drawer scary or sexy? What about all the jeans that now belong in the archives? Is it time to say goodbye to a pile of pieces that are cluttering your life and your drawers?

Marie Kondo was onto something when she told us that things in our life should spark joy. This includes items that even only we see, like the underwear you bought three years ago or the bra that's more like a boob sarong than any real support for the gals.

Today is about creating more space in your head and checking a "nagging" item off your to-do list. Getting started can be the most overwhelming part, BUT once you do even one thing, instantly your list feels lighter.

• Styling Stories •
RENEE WANTED TO BURN HER BRAS

Renee had recently gained 15 pounds. It was that dreadful 15 pounds that happens in your mid-forties and doesn't stop until the hormones have had their fill and resume life in hell where they belong! OMG, I am so sorry, I truly don't know where that rage came from.

Oh wait... It probably stems from the 23 years I have stood next to women, nearly in tears about their bodies, their stomachs, and their hormones. I felt this pain with them, in every appointment, even long before I understood the pain myself.

It never gets easier to see the frustration in someone's eyes as they try on larger clothing sizes than they had ever looked at before, or desperately want to show me photos of who they "used to be."

On the contrary, it's a joy watching them leave feeling better than they have felt in years. It helps heal a part of them. It is possible to love yourself as you are today. To feel and look good in jeans or a dress, just as you are. **Part of dressing on purpose, means dressing for**

yourself today. This means loving and accepting yourself NOW.

As Renee and I stood ready to tackle this 15-pound weight gain, we knew that new bras and underwear had to be part of the conversation. We decided to go up a size through her back, but keep the cup size the same.

Renee and I joked how every morning we both spent 2-3 minutes sifting through old bras that were all worn out, too small, or even just too embarrassing for us to even see ourselves in. It was eating into our precious mornings of coffee and chilling!

And I don't know about you, but I would rather have an extra two minutes sitting and drinking my coffee than sifting through bad bras. What a waste of time.

After Renee bought her new undergarments, I instructed her to go home and spend 10 minutes making sure every bra and sports bra in her drawer actually fit her AND that she really would wear it.

Renee was excellent at following directions, and she herself could barely imagine one more day of such annoyances.

The next morning, after she had cleared out her bra drawer the night before, Renee took a selfie, smiling on the couch sitting for an extra two minutes with her coffee. To be clear, she was fully clothed and not just in her bra, but you get the point. She was thrilled to be lighter emotionally, even if she couldn't be physically. She had done something to help clear her mental headspace, and start her day more purposefully.

When you take the time to cut out the unworn clutter, what remains can all be purposeful.

TRY THIS ON...
ELIMINATE SO YOU CAN ELEVATE

What is one part of your wardrobe that could use some love today? Spend five minutes donating them, tossing them (sad I know), or giving them to someone who could appreciate them.

Do not stop too long to overthink any of this.

Pick a category: jeans, bras, tops, leggings, socks, or underwear. Put your hands on the items as you go through them. Feel the initial gut reaction to the item and move on. Your time is valuable.

The items you put on your body should reflect your magnificent worth. This may seem totally daunting and overwhelming to take on. This is why we are doing one thing at a time.

Think of it as your "focus group" for today. Pick one "focus group" in your closet or wardrobe today.

- » Is it a pair of jeans that no longer flatter you?
- » Is it the sweater with the holes?
- » Is it the collection of dresses that truly don't represent who you are at this point in your life?
- » Is it your bras?
- » Does your underwear need a refresh?

Give yourself the space to realize that you have changed. Even timeless pieces have an expiration date.

⊙ HOW'S EVERYTHING FITTING?

Straightening and cleaning the physical aspects of your life opens up space to focus on the deeply meaningful things to you.

Why is it easy to see this in other areas of our life? Why do we ignore it in our closet?

The most important elements of your life need space to breathe—your family, friends, career, or personal growth.

Knowing your clothing fits you well allows you to approach the world in a more confident way. You feel a difference when you leave the house feeling good about what you are wearing.

When your drawers are filled with fluff that doesn't fit, you are ignoring or delaying a better version of you. Give yourself permission to get unstuck, and do the one thing today that propels you forward.

Lindsey's Tips
TAKING MY OWN ADVICE

I was packing for a work trip to the Hamptons, where I was hosting a styling event. The biggest one of my career at the time. I was nervous and scattered.

The attire needed for this trip was different from my normal vacay packing. I was quickly tossing clothes into my suitcase, late to be getting on the road, when I noticed a small mark on one of my favorite new shirts—ugh, isn't that always the case? Annoyingly, this top was the key component to my fave outfit for the weekend. This was serious stuff...

I cleaned off the spot with soap and warm water. I placed it on the rack near my front door along with the super cute, cropped jean jacket I had recently purchased. I told myself not to forget these items. I needed them for this important trip out East.

I rushed around gathering my other necessities and headed out the door. It was only when I entered the midtown tunnel, exiting the city, that I realized I had forgotten both the formerly stained shirt that was drying and the cute jacket.

Oh, so annoying! I now had to somehow find time to look for a few things when I arrived at my destination. Not a bad problem to have, but certainly not part of my tight agenda or budget.

The next morning, I hit the shopping trail. As I walked into each store, I thought about my *Happy Closet* back at home and the pieces I had left behind. As I tried things on, I imagined myself wearing them, and asked myself if they really made me feel happy.

Now in the past, as a self-diagnosed, recovering shopaholic, I would just buy everything. Even if it made me semi-happy, I would buy it. Because being semi-happy is better than not happy at all, right? Now, the new me, with the *Happy Closet*, only wants to be really happy. I want my clothes to represent the most badass, brilliant side of me.

As I walked in and out of the stores on Main Street, I found it was much easier to say no to items that I would have previously bought without question.

Thinking of my *Happy Closet* even gave me the confidence to walk out of the store without worrying what the sales people thought of me. This is often a reason people (me) buy things— they feel pressured to purchase or perhaps felt guilted into it. But let me tell you, friend. Ain't nobody got to pay that bill but you.

On one hand, you shouldn't feel like you have to buy something. On the other hand...You shouldn't be afraid to take a risk when someone suggests something for you, that you may have not had the confidence to see for yourself.

I never thought that having a *Happy Closet* would actually help me spend LESS money. I also loved seeing a more decisive version of me in action. To this day, I enjoy wearing the few things I bought on that trip.

I spent half the money I planned to, and got double the amount of joy.

DAY 10

I'M WITH THE BAND

This is it. You made it to Day 10. You have seen what it's like to focus on yourself for ten days straight. To feel your enhanced life when you live and dress on purpose.

Now I ask, have you had fun?

Our appearance and self-confidence can be heavy issues. We all have stories and a history with ourselves that only we can understand.

The pain points of the morning can't be solved in 10 days. The daily practices are about gaining awareness and finding new value in yourself.

The opportunity for you to expand is endless. You are an unbelievable gift in this world, and you deserve to show up that way.

I remember a story that reinforced this belief for me.

I struggled with infertility for many years and will most likely fight the battle through menopause. A friend and I were chatting one day.

She mentioned that a mutual acquaintance of ours was pregnant. I suppose I was oddly surprised this woman was having a baby. I replied to her, "Wow, that must be a miracle child."

She replied, "Aren't they all?"

It was like a wave washed over me. Yes, yes every child and human is a miracle.

So listen, my miraculous friend. You deserve to look and feel confident every day. Your workout clothes can be adorable, your blouse can be chic, your jeans can be insanely cute, and your energy can be powerful.

This is not about the money you spend, but about the purposeful choice to spend time on yourself.

As you read today's practice, keep this in mind and let's have some fun.

TRY THIS ON...
LET'S GET LOUD

Today you are going to set aside 10 minutes for picking out your clothes. If this means you need to get up 10 minutes earlier, or ask your family to support this time for you, then please do so. These few minutes are going to be just about you.

This morning you are getting dressed with the energy of your favorite band cheering you on!

First task: Turn on some music. LOUD (but not loud enough to disturb your neighbors or sleeping children). I wouldn't want a noise complaint to disturb our precious morning dance together!!

Pretend as if this music is being played just for you. They are singing to you, playing your favorite song, inspiring you today, showing you all the amazing possibilities that are JUST FOR YOU.

As you get ready, reach for your most colorful underwear (you should have attended to this yesterday), the best bra you have, and then head to your shoe wall.

As you know, I always start my outfit choice with first choosing what shoes to step into. If you like your "kicks" each day and if you feel comfortably chic from your toes up, I believe you can't be that far off from fabulous.

I love a dressy sneaker, great flat, or block heel. My days of stilettos have passed but they hold a place in my heart forever. There is absolutely a way to wear a comfortable and stylish shoe.

If you want to pull up your "Influencer of Your Own Life" album from Day 2, please do so. It can help inspire your outfit today!

After you have decided on your shoes, walk past the black leggings in your closet. Now decide if you want to wear a pair of jeans or a dress today.

As you make these choices, remember the music in the background is playing JUST FOR YOU.

Do a little dip and shake as you dive into your wardrobe, it's ok to be cheesy today. As you reach for your blouse or sweater, indulgently imagine that you are going backstage after the concert. You will get to meet the band. You wouldn't want to wear something you weren't excited about if you were headed to meet Beyonce, Justin Timberlake or Taylor Swift, would you? (Excuse my millennial showing here.)

Pick something that inspires you like this music does.

Think back to the things you learned on the previous days. Are you picking something you love? Or are you holding yourself back from wearing a coveted item?

Notice if you are conveniently ignoring the items you haven't worn in years and won't wear again. (In that case, casually grab it and give it away today!)

Think of the memories you can make in your FAB outfit today. Wear it with excited anticipation of the great day ahead, and hear the music of the world playing just for you.

Adorn yourself with beautiful earrings or a necklace to frame that face of yours! Grab the bag you save for "special nights out." Wear the lipstick that makes your eyes pop. Be as vibrant as the world around you.

Nature does not show up in black and white. The mountains around the world don't hide their magnificent color, and neither should you.

Now stop and take a look in the mirror.

Thank yourself for taking the time for you. Look at your reflection in the mirror and the beautiful life you have built, AND continue to build. Breathe in the courage you have faced, and find peace in the adversity you have overcome throughout the years.

This song is for YOU, my powerful friend. You are living the life you have always dreamed of and now you are showing up on purpose too.

I am so proud of you, but more importantly, you should be proud of yourself.

The music is playing just for you.

Dancing and singing in the mirror is optional, yet encouraged.

PART 3
THE PURPOSEFUL, SUCCESSFUL, FASHIONABLE YOU

THIS IS NOT GOODBYE, THIS IS YOUR GOOD MORNING...

You may think that because I am a stylist, I am judging your outfit and what you wear.

I often hear, "I had to dress more fab today because I knew I was going to see YOU, Lindsey!" I appreciate that. I appreciate that people think my opinion matters and that it would somehow help shape someone's day in a positive way..

But I don't actually care what you are wearing. I care that YOU care what you are wearing. That is what matters to me.

It doesn't have to be the most stylish outfit, the most couture designer or current trend. It's all about YOU...

- » Did you take the time to care for yourself today?
- » Did you notice that how you show up matters?
- » Did you feel good about yourself today?
- » Did you choose an outfit that helps you HIDE or helps your HIGHLIGHT all that's wonderful about you?

When you deliberately present yourself to the world with intention—as you see yourself and as you wish to be seen—something truly magical happens. You become a beacon, a guiding light, that beckons and draws toward you everything you want to manifest in your life.

Love. Happiness. Success. Fun. Freedom. Joy. Purpose.

And like everything in life, it all starts with YOU. With your mindset, your self-awareness, your self-confidence, and appreciation of the wonderful you, you are today and what you can become.

What you wear is the spotlight you place on yourself—for yourself and everyone around you. When you create a *Happy Closet*, what you are really doing is generating an energy that will fuel you, every day.

Your *Happy Closet* is the place you go to make choices about who you are at that very moment. And because you are a dynamic, evolving force of nature, your *Happy Closet* will evolve and change with you.

It will reflect who you are today, and invite you to create who you can be tomorrow.

Some of the first thoughts you have about yourself each day are as you are getting dressed.

Those words should be the highest form of positivity towards yourself. Love what you wear. Push yourself to expand out of the black leggings and into the color this world has to offer.

This is your beginning. This is the awakening of your beautiful, purposeful life. This is the first step of creating the essential habit of taking the time to find meaning in your day.

Nestled within the fabrics of that beautiful blouse, cozy sweater, or power suit—this is where it begins for you.

As you continue on your journey, I want you to dream of what's possible...

- » Find the purpose in your day, every day.
- » Become the influencer of YOUR own life, and envision your dream wardrobe before it may even exist.
- » Create your *Happy Closet*.
- » Come out of the dark and live out loud in color.
- » Wear the clothing you were inspired to buy.
- » Start showing up as the next version of your evolution.
- » Compliment the beauty in people around you.
- » Spend a few minutes clearing your space for MORE greatness to come.
- » SING AT THE TOP OF YOUR LUNGS like the band is playing JUST FOR YOU!

Thank you for sharing the last 10 days with me. I have been wanting to share this story for as long as I can remember.

Because what I know for you is THIS...

You are a star. The world exists for you. Take up space. Do not let anyone tell you that you are too much. You are enough.

Remember this, put it into action. No matter how busy you are.

You get to start fresh today, you get to choose how big you want to live.

You are here for a reason. It's time to SHOW UP like it.

When you confidently face the world, the world will rise to meet you.

When you show up, the world is waiting to greet and embrace YOU.

After all... You can't leave the house naked, and the world is waiting for you, so let's live and dress on purpose.

AUTHOR'S NOTE

Dear Reader,

Thank you for joining this journey with me. I had so much fun writing this book. It awakened something in me that had been silent for many years. I hope you found some hidden piece of yourself here too.

As one of the top retail luxury retail stylists in the country, I have had great success in my career. I spend my days helping women show up and live on purpose.

Dressing women is my superpower. I know how clothing fits and can style someone perfectly from head to toe with one glance. I can accurately guess your shoe size over the phone (don't know how).

I often think that we are given the tools to help others learn the things that we ourselves have struggled with. For me, that was confidence. Growing up, I didn't have confidence in myself. So I have dedicated my life to helping women find theirs.

Sometimes, we lose ourselves in the joy of our lives. We often believe that when everyone else around us is happy, that is enough.

My mission is to change the way women approach their day, starting with their wardrobe. I show women what it means to believe in themselves first. The rest will follow.

Fashionably Yours,

Lindsey

ACKNOWLEDGMENTS

Thank you: Jason, my love.

Bryce, my world.

Mom and Dad, for letting me be me. I am here because of you two. I love you.

Jan and Richard Prifold, for being the best.

My amazing coach Jenny Aiello, an incredible bright light on my path.

My mentors and besties who helped edit, listen, and inspire (over and over)—Marla, Miranda, and the Four with Mary, Deb, and Vick.

Wendy and Ken Goodrich for the inspo to be the influencer of my own life, shared over margaritas in Mexico.

Nancy Bruce, for your genius.

Rachelle Borer, for your patience and detail-oriented, editing mind. I love how strangers can become friends.

To all the women I have dressed before:

You are powerful, and you make me powerful.

You are the reason I am here and the inspiration for this book. Thank you.

ABOUT THE AUTHOR

Lindsey Bernay is a leading fashion expert and visionary in the styling industry. She has outfitted thousands of women, including busy moms, high-profile executives, and celebrities. Lindsey has been featured in international documentaries, news segments, and in print and fashion magazines. Most days you can find her walking up Fifth Avenue in New York City, where she resides with her partner Jason and their daughter.

Follow her @lindseybernaystyles where she shares wardrobe tips, chronicles her fashion events, and encourages her thousands of followers to live and dress "on purpose."